CALLIMACHUS' IAMBI

MNEMOSYNE

BIBLIOTHECA CLASSICA BATAVA

COLLEGERUNT

W. DEN BOER • A. D. LEEMAN • W. J. VERDENIUS

BIBLIOTHECAE FASCICULOS EDENDOS CURAVIT

W. J. VERDENIUS, HOMERUSLAAN 53, ZEIST

SUPPLEMENTUM QUINQUAGESIMUM NONUM

D. L. CLAYMAN

CALLIMACHUS' IAMBI

LUGDUNI BATAVORUM E. J. BRILL MCMLXXX

CALLIMACHUS' IAMBI

BY

D. L. CLAYMAN

LEIDEN E. J. BRILL 1980

ISBN 90 04 06063 4

For C.E.C.
G.C.C. and T.E.C.

TABLE OF CONTENTS

ACKNOWLEDGEMENTS

It is a pleasure to acknowledge the aid of those who helped bring this work to fruition. First and foremost is Lloyd W. Daly, Professor Emeritus of the University of Pennsylvania, who first introduced me to Callimachus and helped to launch this study as a doctoral dissertation submitted to the University of Pennsylvania in 1972. Through the years he has continued to provide guidance and inspiration. I owe him more than I can say. Prof. L. E. Rossi of Rome, the late Prof. H. Gundert of Freiburg and my colleagues Prof. H. Hansen and Prof. J. Van Sickle read versions of the manuscript in its entirety and made many valuable criticisms. A. Hickey patiently re-checked all of the references. The remaining errors are all may own.

This research was supported by a grant from the City University of New York PSC-BHE Research Award Program.

ABBREVIATIONS

Dawson	C. M. Dawson, "The *Iambi* of Callimachus," *Yale Classical Studies* 11 (1950) 1-168.
D.³	E. Diehl, *Anthologia Lyrica Graeca* ³ (Leipzig 1949-1952).
Pf. I	R. Pfeiffer, *Callimachus* Vol. I (Oxford 1949).
Pf. II	R. Pfeiffer, *Callimachus* Vol. II (Oxford 1953).
Puelma	M. Puelma-Piwonka, *Lucilius und Kallimachos* (Dissert. Zurich 1947).
Schn.	O. Schneider, *Callimachea* ² (Leipzig 1870-1873).
W.	M. L. West, *Iambi et Elegi Graeci* Vol. I (Oxford 1971).

Abbreviations for the names of journals correspond with those in *L'Année philologique*. Abbreviations for the titles of ancient texts correspond with those in Liddell, Scott, Jones, *Greek-English Lexicon* and Lewis and Short, *A Latin Dictionary*.

INTRODUCTION

History of the Text

Although Callimachus enjoyed a towering reputation in antiquity, by the beginning of the thirteenth century the largest part of his work, including the *Iambi*, had disappeared. Word by word, line by line, the remains of the original text have been painstakingly reassembled. The story of the reconstruction of the *Iambi* is a testimony to the persistence and ingenuity of several generations of classical scholars who have helped one another to recover the traces of Callimachus' art.

The story begins with Politian who first collected a few fragments of the lost texts that have survived in the works of ancient commentators in the first book of his *Miscellanea* (1489). In the early part of the 16th century Ianus Parrhasius published some testimonia and fragments of the *Aitia*. These collections were reprinted together with the extant *Hymns* and *Epigrams* in the second edition of Stephanus (1577).[1] Later editors of the *Hymns* were able to accumulate more citations. The first to include a fragment of the *Iambi* was Vulcanius (1584), whose collection of 56 fragments was reprinted by Fabri (1675) with 53 others garnered herself from different sources.[2] Fabri's collection includes a second fragment of the *Iambi*.[3]

Graevius (1697) later augmented the work of Vulcanius and Fabri with fragments collected by Spanheim and Bentley.[4] Bentley identified 25 fragments of the Iambi among a total of 417.[5]

---

[1] Angelus Politianus, *Miscellanea* (Florence 1489). H. Stephanus, *Callimachi Cyrenaei Hymni et Epigrammata* (Geneva 1577).

A short discussion of previous texts of the fragments of Callimachus can be found in R. Pfeiffer, *Callimachus* II (Oxford 1953) xliii-l. On the late survival cf. xxxiv-xxxviii.

[2] B. Vulcanius, *Callimachi Cyrenaei Hymni et Epigrammata Fragmenta quae Exstant* (Antwerp 1584). The fragment is 191.9-11 Pf. = 86 Schn. A. Fabri, *Callimachi Cyrenaei Hymni Epigrammata et Fragmenta* (Paris 1675) 153-167.

[3] Fabri, XXII = 192.1-3 Pf. = 87 Schn..

[4] T. Graevius, *Callimachi Hymni Epigrammata et Fragmenta* (Ultrajecti 1697).

[5] See Pf. II, xlvi-v for an evaluation of the charge that Bentley pirated his collection from an unpublished manuscript of Th. Stanley.

Among the 25 are pieces written in choliambic and pure iambic
trimeters attributed to Callimachus but not necessarily identified
by their sources as extracts from the *Iambi* or *Choliambi*. No
epodic verses are admitted. There are about 60 iambic verses
altogether. Bentley's attributions, order, and numbering were
retained in subsequent editions by J. Ernesti (1761), C. J. Blomfield
(1815), and O. Schneider (1870-73).[6]

The information about the *Iambi* which could be gleaned from
these fragments is neatly summarized in Susemihl's account.

> In der Einleitung zu seiner "Iamboi" betitelten Sammlung
> iambischer und choliambischer Gedichte scheint er sich
> als einen Hipponax redivivus, aber von milderem Auftreten
> bezeichnet zu haben, und so waren sie denn, wenn auch herbe
> Polemik, z.B. gegen Euhemeros, in ihnen nicht fehlte, doch
> sehr gemischten Inhalts. Zu den choliambischen gehörten
> auch Fabeln.[7]

Bentley and his successors exhausted the ancient sources, but
to our great fortune the number of extant fragments was soon
increased dramatically by the discovery of important papyrus
texts, starting in 1904 with *P. Oxy.* 661.[8] This text contains the
beginnings and ends of lines from two columns of epodes, iambic
trimeters alternating with trochaic lines, in the Doric dialect.
Although the dialect excludes the most obvious candidate, Archilochus, only Blass was astute enough to recognize Callimachus'
claim to authorship.[9] After the discovery and publication of the
Diegeseis in 1934, R. Pfeiffer was able to certify that these fragments belong to lines 11-25 and 39-51 of *Iamb* 7.[10]

In the following winter (1905), a more spectacular manuscript
was discovered at Oxyrhynchus published in 1910 as *P. Oxy.*

---

[6] J. Ernesti, *Callimachi: Hymni Epigrammata et Fragmenta* (Lugduni
Batavorum 1761). C. J. Blomfield, *Callimachi quae Supersunt* (London
1815). O. Schneider, *Callimachea*[2] (Leipzig 1870-1873).

[7] F. Susemihl, *Geschichte der griechischen Litteratur in der Alexandriner
Zeit* I (Leipzig 1891) 356.

[8] B. P. Grenfell and A. S. Hunt (eds.), *The Oxyrhynchus Papyri* 4 (1904)
62-64.

[9] *P. Oxy.* 661 (above n. 8) 62. The claim was denied by Wilamowitz
(Pf. II, xvii).

[10] R. Pfeiffer, "Die neuen ΔΙΗΓΗΣΕΙΣ zu Kallimachosgedichten,"
Sitzungsberichte der bayerischen Akademie der Wissenschaften (1934) 10, 23-30.

1011.[11] It consists of seven partly mutilated folia and some smaller fragments of Callimachean poetry. The first folium contains the story of Acontius and Cydippe known to have come from the third book of the *Aitia*; the second contains the epilogue of the *Aitia* followed by a subscription and a new title, "Iamboi." The appearance in the text that follows of lines securely attested by other sources as *Iambi* of Callimachus corroborates the title and confirms the authorship.

In the original publication Hunt arranged folia 2-6 with the aid of numbers written at the top of folia 1, 3, and 5. He organized the fragments, some 334 lines, into four iambic poems and one trochaic poem which he placed last on account of its different meter. These fragments are now designated as *Iambi* 1-4, 12 and 13.

Hunt's original organization was maintained by R. Pfeiffer when he re-edited the fragments in 1921, by E. Cahen in his edition of 1922, and by E. Lobel in 1934.[12] Lobel was able to offer improved readings made possible by the use of ultraviolet light. He was the first to recognize that the fragments of *P. Oxy.* 1363 which had been published in 1915 [13] belong to folium 2 of *P. Oxy.* 1011 as also does frag. 11 of *P. Oxy.* 1011 itself.

In addition to fragments of the text, papyri were discovered which contain commentary on the *Iambi*. The earliest of these is *PSI* 1094, the so-called Scholia Florentina, which contains a detailed commentary on a small portion of Iamb 1.[14] Of far greater importance are the self-styled *Diegeseis* which were discovered in 1934 by A. Vogliano and published soon afterwards by M. Norsa and G. Vitelli.[15] Three years later Vogliano produced a revised version which has served as the basis of all subsequent texts.[16]

This papyrus contains a prose summary of the third and fourth books of the *Aitia* followed by descriptions of seventeen shorter poems or all of which are *Iambi*. Each of these seventeen is intro-

---

[11] A. S. Hunt (ed.) with help from G. Murray and Ul. von Wilamowitz-Moellendorf, *The Oxyrhynchus Papyri* 7 (1910) 15-82.

[12] R. Pfeiffer, *Callimachi Fragmenta Nuper Reperta* (Bonn 1921).

E. Cahen, *Callimaque* (Paris 1922).

E. Lobel, "The Choliambi of Callimachus in *P. Oxy.* 1011," *Hermes* 69 (1934) 167-178.

[13] B. P. Grenfell and A. S. Hunt, *The Oxyrhynchus Papyri* 11 (1915) 90-92.

[14] G. Vitelli, *Papiri della societa italiana* 9 (1929) 157-164.

[15] M. Norsa and G. Vitelli, ΔΙΗΓΗΣΕΙΣ *di poemi di Callimaco in un papiro di Tebtynis*, Papyri della R. Università di Milano (Firenze 1934).

[16] A. Vogliano (ed.), *Papyri della R. Università di Milano* 1 (1937) 66-173.

duced by its opening line, as are the brief outlines of the *Hecale*, the *Hymn to Zeus*, and part of the *Hymn to Apollo* which follow. With this information P. Maas was able to reassign the lines of folia 2-5 of *P. Oxy.* 1011. The First *Iamb* clearly should end at line 159; the second, at line 173; the third at line 205; and the fourth at line 303.[17]

Scholars readily agreed on the new line assignments for *Iambi* 1-4. There has been much controversy, however, over the number, order, and meter of the other *Iambi*. Maas himself separated the first four stichic choliambic poems from the eight poems which follow. He believed these eight to be epodic. The distinction between a group of stichic poems and a group of epodes was maintained by A. Rostagni, although he included the fifth poem in the stichic group and also the thirteenth which in his estimation had been misplaced by the *Dieg.*[18] He would have the six remaining "epodes" follow after the stichic poems. The trochaic poem (fr. 202) would come last and would serve as a neat transition to the four melic poems which conclude the group of seventeen.

These last four poems are not given a separate title by the *Dieg.*, but they have been distinguished from the *Iambi* on the basis of their meter and subject matter. They were first associated with the *Mele* of Callimachus by R. Pfeiffer in 1923.[19] Pfeiffer defended this identification in his own assessment of the *Dieg.*, where he describes them as, "εἰδύλλια, Einzelgedichte mit Einzeltiteln: πρὸς τοὺς ὡραίους (?) in Phalaceen, παννυχίς ... in euripideischen Vierzehnsilbern, ἐκθέωσις 'Αρσινόης in Archebuleen, Βράγχος in choriambischen Pentametern.[20] Pfeiffer maintained that these poems never formed a separate book of their own, but were collected together in a larger edition of Callimachus' poetry. This hypothesis accounts for the fact that none of the fragments has ever been cited as being found ἐν μέλεσι.

Pfeiffer did not retain Rostagni's and Maas's simple three meter

---

[17] P. Maas, rev. of ΔΙΗΓΗΣΕΙΣ *di poemi di Callimaco in un papiro di Tebtynis* in *Gnomon* 10 (1934) 436-439.

[18] A. Rostagni, "Le nuove ΔΙΗΓΗΣΕΙΣ e l'ordinamento dei carmi di Callimaco," *RFIC* N.S. 12 (1934) 289-312.

[19] R. Pfeiffer, *Callimachi Fragmenta Nuper Reperta* ² (Bonn 1923) which includes fragments of these poems found earlier in *P. Oxy.* 1793. A group of Callimachean poems designated by the title *Mele* are cited by the Suda s.v. Καλλίμαχος = test. 1, Pf. II, xcv.

[20] R. Pfeiffer, *Sitzungsberichte* (above n. 10) 43.

scheme, but instead viewed the *Iambi* as containing a variety of meters, "Das Iambenbuch bietet, wenn man nicht konstruiert, eine bunte Reihe von metrischen Formen, die sich allerdings alle im Rahmen der von den ionischen Iambographoi Archilochos und Hipponax gegebenen Muster halten, vielleicht mit neuen epodischen Kombinationen." [21] He followed Rostagni, however in associating the twelfth trochaic poem with the *Mele*, and accepted the consequent conclusion that the thirteenth poem had been misplaced by the *Dieg*. This rationalization allowed him to preserve Hunt's arrangement of folia 6 and 7 of *P. Oxy.* 1011.

The theme of variety was taken up again by G. Coppola who was the first to attempt a large scale reassessment of all of the Callimachean fragments in the light of the evidence of the *Dieg*.[22] Coppola's comparison of the *Iambi* to the inherently various *Latina Satura* has become the keynote in modern criticism of these poems.

In his organization of the fragments of the *Iambi* Coppola parted ways with Pfeiffer and Rostagni. He insisted on following the testimony of the *Dieg*., admitting the twelfth poem as an *Iamb* in spite of its trochaic meter and rejecting Hunt's arrangement of folia 6 and 7 of *P. Oxy.* 1011.[23] In addition to the trochaic twelfth, Coppola also wished to include the fourteenth poem, in phalaeceans, because of its satiric tone. This last suggestion has been followed only by Lavagnini.[24]

A. Körte shared Coppola's faith in the *Dieg*. but drew from his faith more radical conclusions about the number and order of the poems.[25] Körte not only followed the order of the *Dieg*. in the placement of trochaic *Iamb* 12 before iambic 13, he also followed the *Dieg*. in including all seventeen poems between the *Aitia* and the *Hecale* under the title *Iamboi*. Körte could see no reason to exclude the final four poems on the basis of meter in view of the wide variety of meters already present in poems 1-13. The fifteenth

---

[21] R. Pfeiffer, *Sitzungsberichte* (above n. 10) 42.

[22] G. Coppola, *Cirene e il nuovo Callimaco*, R. Accademia delle scienze dell' Istituto di Bologna, Classe di scienze morali (Bologna 1935).

[23] G. Coppola (above n. 22) 100.

[24] B. Lavagnini, "Osservazioni ai *Giambi* di Callimaco," *Atti di R. Accademia di scienze lettere e belle arti di Palermo* Ser. 3, 19 (1935) 393-402. Lavagnini is impressed by the observation that the three final poems follow a *prooimion* εἰς τοὺς Διοσκούρους καὶ Ἑλένην (Dieg. X 6) 398.

[25] A. Körte, "Literarische Texte mit Ausschluss der christlichen," *Archiv für Papyrusforschung und verwandte Gebiete* 13 (1938) 78-132 esp. 87-89.

poem in his estimation is itself an epode and therefore closely connected with the preceding iambic epodes. To defend his metrical theories Körte pointed out that there is no solid evidence that Callimachus ever wrote a book of *Mele*; no fragment of Callimachus has ever been cited as coming from the *Mele*; and that the story of Branchus, told in the seventeenth poem, the last of the alleged *Mele*, is in fact cited by Clement of Alexandria (Strom. V. 8, 48 Vol. II p. 359 St.) as narrated Καλλιμάχου ἐν ἰάμβοις.

Körte's arguments were immediately accepted by Cahen and attacked by Vogliano in his new and definitive edition of the *Dieg.*[26] On the subject of meter, Vogliano successfully demonstrates that 15 is not an epode and therefore has no significant ties to the earlier poems. On the question of title, Vogliano notes that the existence of Callimachean *Mele* is attested by the *Suda* whose general confusion does not necessarily discount this evidence. Körte's argument that no fragment of Callimachus has ever been cited this title is an argument *ex silentio* and therefore to be distrusted. Furthermore, the copyist of the *Dieg.* omitted either a title or a subscription after the *Hekale* and so it is not inconceivable that he omitted a title before the *Mele* as well.

The best argument against Vogliano's proof that the seventeenth poem on Branchus has been cited ἐν ἰάμβοις was made not by Vogliano, but by one of Körte's staunchest supporters, C. Gallavotti.[27] In spite of his desire to vindicate Körte, Gallavotti conceded that the citation of Clement of Alexandria does not necessarily refer to the seventeenth poem. Clement merely indicates that a particular detail of the myth of Branchus is recorded in Callimachus' *Iambi*. This notice could easily refer to the Branchus mentioned in *Iamb* 4.28-29. A more recently discovered fragment of the seventeenth poem, *P. Oxy.* 2172 seems to support this view.[28]

A detailed summary of the first stages of this controversy about the order and number of the *Iambi* can be found in H.

---

[26] E. Cahen, "L'Oeuvre poétique de Callimaque: Documents nouveaux," *REG* 48 (1935) 279-321.

[27] C. Gallavotti, "Il libro dei *Giambi* di Callimaco," *Antiquitas* I (1946) 11-22.

[28] Gallavotti accepts all of Körte's other arguments in favor of 17 *Iambi* and adds several of his own including a comparison between Callimachus' *Iambi* and Horace's 17 *Epodes* and a papyrological argument based on the belief that *P. Oxy.* 2172 which contains the last verse of the seventeenth poem is part of the end of a papyrus volume.

Herter's invaluable bibliography of 1937.[29] In recent years, scholars have generally agreed on following the order of the poems set by the *Diegeseis*, but the debate on the number of iambic poems still continues. Those who support Körte in accepting seventeen *Iambi* now include M. Puelma-Piwonka, A. Ardizzoni and L. E. Rossi.[30] Those who favor the number 13 include R. Pfeiffer, C. Dawson, and myself.[31]

In my estimation, the most compelling argument for the unity of the 13 poems lies not in metrical considerations nor in the presence or absence of titles in the ancient manuscripts, but in the perception that the first 13 poems are strongly unified in theme and outlook and the thirteenth poem is essentially a summary of ideas and images which are developed in the 12 preceding poems. This argument was first made in an article which appeared in 1976, and is further developed in Chapter 1 which follows.[32] I have become persuaded since that time that the four poems which follow the original *Iambi*, call them *Mele* or whatever, were added to a manuscript of the *Iambi* in antiquity in order to fill out the "book," and that the total of 17 poems was known at Rome. Whether these were added by the poet himself in an omnibus edition which he made late in life,[33] or by a copyist, they were in place by the time the poems came to Rome and were seen by Catullus,[34] who wrote iambic hendecasyllables and Horace who wrote 17 *Epodes*.

While the controversy about the number and order of the *Iambi* was in progress, many other bits and pieces of papyri were dis-

---

[29] H. Herter, "Bericht über die Literatur zur hellenistischen Dichtung aus den Jahren 1921-1935," *Jahresbericht über die Fortschritte der klassischen Altertumswissenschaft* 255 (1937) 65-226, esp. 161.

[30] M. Puelma-Piwonka, *Lucilius und Kallimachos* (Dissert. Zurich 1947); A. Ardizzoni, "Considerazioni sulla struttura del libro dei *Giambi* di Callimaco," *Miscellanea di studi alessandrini* in memoria di Augusto Rostagni (Torino 1963) 257-262. (Ardizzoni's arguments rely heavily on Körte and Gallavotti); L. E. Rossi, in conversation.

[31] Pf. II, xxxvi; C. M. Dawson, "The Iambi of Callimachus," *YCS* 11 (1950) 1-168 esp. 132-133.

[32] "Callimachus' Thirteenth *Iamb*: The Last Word," *Hermes* 104 (1976) 29-35.

[33] Pf. II xxxiii-xxxviii; Dawson 145-148.

[34] Perhaps Catullus was introduced to Callimachus by Parthenius. See W. Clausen, "Callimachus and Latin Poetry," *GRBS* 5 (1964) 181-196, and R. Pfeiffer, "A Fragment of Parthenius' *Arete*," *C.Q.* 37 (1943) 23-32. On the *Iambi* at Rome see Chapt. IV below.

covered and identified as containing new fragments of the poems. In 1933 Norsa and Vitelli published some epodic fragments that they identified as Archilochean.[35] Although they recorded a suggestion by V. Bartoletti that the poems resemble some of Callimachus', especially fr. 98[a] Schn. = 195.23-29, they dismissed the idea as "sfuggito." Pasquali and Pfeiffer, however, gave it early support.[36] After the publication of the *Dieg.*, E. Cahen was able to identify the fragments positively as part of *Iamb* 5 (fr. 195.20-34).[37]

Column II of this same papyrus also contains fragments of the first twenty-one lines of *Iamb* 6. Better preserved pieces were found later in *P. Oxy.* 2171 which is part of the same manuscript.[38] The texts were joined and re-edited by Pfeiffer in 1941.[39]

Other papyrus finds include *P. Ryl.* 485 which yields small fragments of *Iambi* 4 and 5 (fr. 194.115-117 and 195.1-7), *P. Oxy.* 2215 which contains additions to *Iambi* 3 and 4 (fr. 193.5-24 and 194.14-21), and *P. Oxy.* 2218 which contains the first 6 lines of *Iamb* 12 (fr. 202.1-6).[40] Most recently, there has been a major addition to *Iamb* 12 from *P. Mich.* inv. 4947.[41]

In spite of this proliferation of material, there have been only three modern texts of the *Iambi*. The earliest was done by C. Gallavotti, in 1946.[42] In addition to the text, Gallavotti includes an extensive apparatus filled with many ingenious hypotheses for readings, an introduction covering such topics as papyrus sources, subject matter, date and manner of composition, a table of meter and prosody, substantial indices, a large bibliography, and finally an Italian translation. Impressive as the work is, C. Dawson set

---

[35] M. Norsa and G. Vitelli, "Frammenti di Archiloco in un papiro della società italiana," *Atene e Roma* ser. 3, 1 (1933) 7-12. Later *PSI* 1216 col. I 30-45.

[36] G. Pasquali, "Sul nuovo epodo fiorentino II. Archiloco o Callimaco?" *SIFC* N.S. 3, 10 (1932-1933) 169-175 and R. Pfeiffer, "Ein Epodenfragment aus dem Iambenbuche des Kallimachos," *Philologus* 88 (1933) 265-271.

[37] E. Cahen (above, n. 26).

[38] E. Lobel (ed.), *The Oxyrhynchus Papyri* 18 (1941) 56-62 and addenda 183-184. This text also yielded fragments of *Iambi* 4 and 7.

[39] R. Pfeiffer, "The Measurements of Zeus at Olympia," *JHS* 61 (1941) 1-5.

[40] C. H. Roberts, *Catalogue of the Greek Papyri in the John Rylands Library* 3 (1938) 97-98; E. Lobel (ed.), *The Oxyrhynchus Papyri* 19 (1948) 38-41, 46.

[41] 202.57-70. C. Bonner, "A New Fragment of Callimachus," *Aegyptus* 31 (1951) 133-137, later appearing in Pf. II among the addenda, 118-119.

[42] C. Gallavotti, *Callimaco: Il libro dei Giambi* (Napoli 1946).

out four years later to make another independent text.[43] In Dawson's edition the text of each poem is followed by an English translation, a text and translation of the relevant sections of the *Dieg.* and a short discussion of the contents of both. The work is crowned by an exhaustive bibliography and an illuminating discussion of the *Iambi* as a collection.

Dawson was not able to make use of Pfeiffer's monumental edition of all of the fragments of Callimachus which appeared almost simultaneously.[44] Although Pfeiffer used the same papyrus material as Dawson, his text looks somewhat fuller because he is a bolder emendator. Pfeiffer's edition contains a full apparatus and Latin notes which reprint all relevant testimonia. Volume II published in 1953 contains extensive introductory material and indices. All references to fragment and line numbers in the text below are made to Pfeiffer's edition, which has set a new standard of excellence in modern scholarship. Trypanis' Loeb edition of 1958 is based on Pfeiffer's text. Trypanis has added some supplements, emendations and a tolerable English translation of the major passages.[45]

Outside of these editions, scholarship dealing with the *Iambi* has appeared largely in occasional articles, with the important exception of M. Puelma-Piwonka's *Lucilius und Kallimachos.*[46]

---

[43] C. Dawson (above, n. 31).

[44] R. Pfeiffer, *Callimachus* I (Oxford 1949).

[45] C. A. Trypanis, *Callimachus: Fragments*, Loeb Classical Library (Cambridge, Mass. 1958).

[46] See Dawson (above n. 57) 152-157 for an extensive bibliography to which may now be added A. Ardizzoni, "Callimaco Ipponatteo," *Annali della facoltà di lettere filosofia e magistero dell' Università di Cagliari* 28 (1960) 7-20; W. Bühler, "Archilochos und Kallimachos," *Archiloque*, Fondation Hardt Entretiens 10 (Genève 1963) 225-247; L. Deubner, "Die *Saturae* des Ennius und die *Jamben* des Kallimachos," *RhM*. 96 (1953) 289-292; H. Diller, "Zu Kallimachos," *Hermes* 90 (1962) 119-121; R. Kassel, "Kleinigkeiten zu den Kallimachos-Fragmenten," *RhM*. 101 (1958) 235-238; F. Lapp, *De Callimachi Cyrenaei Tropis et Figures* (Dissert. Bonn 1965); H. Lloyd-Jones, "Callimachus fr. 191.62," *CR* N.S. 17 (1967) 125-127; G. Luck, "Kids and Wolves: Callimachus fr. 202.69-70," *CQ* N.S. 9 (1959) 34-37; M. Puelma, "Kallimachos-Interpretationen," *Philologus* 101 (1957) 90-100, 247-268; B. R. Rees, "Callimachus, Iambus I 9-11," *CR* N.S. 11 (1961) 1-3; D. A. Tsiribas, "Καλλιμάχου Ἴαμβος κατὰ Εὐθυδήμου," *Athena* 59 (1955) 150-174; and any other titles mentioned in the notes above which are dated after 1949.

In addition to the articles listed above the *Iambi* are considered briefly by W. Wimmel, *Kallimachos in Rom*, Hermes Einzelschriften 16 (Leiden 1960) as they relate to his discussion of the poet's "apology" and they are mentioned

Puelma's fascinating book is an elaborate effort to define an iambic *Gattungsidee* which is shared by both poets. The *Iambi* receive extensive treatment both individually and as a group. Unfortunately, Puelma has emended the text extensively in ways which promote his own occasionally idiosyncratic interpretations.

Although our knowledge of the *Iambi* has increased so dramatically in this century, there has not been to date any completely satisfactory study of these poems as a literary phenomenon. Dawson made a significant beginning, and it is his work that is the foundation of this present effort. The question at issue here is this: What is the place of Callimachus' *Iambi* in the development of the iambic genre? An answer to this question requires looking forward, backward and inward. Chapter I describes the *Iambi* individually and as a collection. Chapter II contains a study of the *Iambi* and the work of earlier iambic poets. Chapter III assesses the place of the *Iambi* in their Alexandrian milieu. Chapter IV surveys their influence at Rome. When the nature of the *Iambi* is revealed and their role in the development of the genre, some general truths emerge about Callimachus' art and his place in literary history.

------

here and there by G. Capovilla whose labyrinthine *Callimaco*, Studia Philol. 10 (Roma 1967) lacks an index, making the references extremely difficult to locate.

CHAPTER ONE

THE *IAMBI* INDIVIDUALLY AND TOGETHER

Iamb I (fr. 191)

'Ακούσαθ' 'Ιππώνακτος· οὐ γὰρ ἀλλ' ἥκω
ἐκ τῶν ὅκου βοῦν κολλύβου πιπρήσκουσιν,

Listen to Hipponax. For I have come
from the place where an ox costs a penny,

(191.1-2).

Callimachus begins by exhibiting a re-incarnated Hipponax,
using Hipponax's choliambic meter and a modified form of his
Ionian dialect. Hipponax is haranguing a group of men who are
identified by the *Dieg.* as philologoi, clearly the literati of Ptolemy's
Museum.[1] The scene is set in contemporary Alexandria at the
Great Sarapeum of Parmenio, where Hipponax himself has assembled the scholars (191.9).[2] The appearance of Hipponax's
ghost at the temple of Sarapis both compliments the Ptolemies
who are said to have founded the cult,[3] and implies that the philo-

---

[1] His audience is described by the *Dieg* VI 3 as τοὺς φιλολόγους or τοὺς
φιλοσόφους. Pf. I 163 provides ancient references for the use of both terms
for the members of the Museum.

[2] So the ἱρόν is identified by the *Dieg.* VI 3-4. This would seem to refer
to the great Sarapeum of Parmeniscus which stood outside the walls of
Rhacotis built by Ptolemy III after 247/6 B.C. Pfeiffer has refuted this
view, noting that Euhemerus, a contemporary of King Cassander (317/6-
298/7 B.C.), is depicted in *Iamb* I writing in the temple (191.10-11) which
he could not have been alive to see if it were built by Ptolemy III. Pfeiffer
also rejects the identification of the structure as an older sacellum built
at Rhacotis by Ptolemy I (Tac. *Hist.* 4.84) because it could not possibly
be described as "outside the wall" as it is in 191.9 (Pf. II xxxix-xl).
Pfeiffer's arguments have been met most ingeniously by B. R. Rees,
"Callimachus, *Iambus* I 9-11," *CR* 11 (1961) 1-3, who argues that the
Euhemerus depicted in the Sarapeum may be a statue of Euhemerus, such
as the many statues of Greek poets and philosophers which stood in the
exedra of the Sarapeum in Memphis. If the reference is to a statue of Euhemerus, all of the chronological objections to the ἱρόν's being the Great
Sarapeum disappear and the first *Iamb* at least may be dated very late in
Callimachus' lifetime. This reference is the sole "objective" criterion for
dating the *Iambi*.

[3] Among the ancients, Plut. *Isis and Osiris* 361F and Tac. *Hist.* 4.83-84.
See P. M. Fraser, "Two Studies on the Cult of Serapis in the Hellenistic
World," *Opuscula Atheniensia* 3 (1960) 1-54.

logoi are sick and have come to the temple in the hopes of having
a dream vision which will give them the advice they need in order
to be cured.[4] Hipponax's ghost is the answer to their prayers.

Hipponax begins the proceedings with an observation, no doubt
uncomplimentary, on "men who are now" (191.6). In the next
lines (191.7-9) he mentions Dionysus, the Muses, and Apollo
and summons the crowd to the temple where he delivers a quick
insult to Euhemerus whose statue may have been set up there
(n. 2 below).

ἐς τὸ πρὸ τείχευς ἱρὸν ἀλέες δεῦτε,
οὗ τὸν πάλαι Πάγχαιον ὁ πλάσας Ζᾶνα
γέρων λαλάζων ἄδικα βιβλία ψήχει.

Come all together to the temple before the wall
where the man who invented ancient Panchaian Zeus,
the old babbler, scratches out his impious books.

(191.9-11)

In the fourteen lacunose lines which follow Hipponax refers to
the interior of the building (191.12) and to altars presumably
outside of it (191.14). He swears appropriately by Hades (191.15),
and says something on the subject of literature: Μοῦσα (191.17),
ἴ]αμβον (191.21),]άμετρα (191.23).[5]

At line 26 where continuous text resumes, Hipponax, in his
best iambic manner, compares the philologoi to swarming flies
and wasps (191.26-27) and to citizens of Delphi who snatch for
themselves portions of the victims slaughtered in honor of the
god (191.27-28).[6] One member of the crowd is singled out, an
unnamed bald man, who is in danger of losing his cloak or *tribon*
(191.29-30). The garment suggests that he is a philosopher, probably
a cynic. Philosophers are commonly the butt of jokes in middle
and new comedy (e.g. Menander on the Cynic Crates' *tribon* in
fr. 117-118 K), but this little vignette has an extra dimension

---

[4] Tac. *Hist.* 4.84 says that Sarapis was thought to resemble Asclepius
because he heals sick bodies, and because petitioners receive their instructions
in dreams.

[5] Puelma, 219-220, reconstructs these lines so that they become a catalog
of the assembled literati grouped by genre.

[6] Schol. Flor. 15 tells how Aesop was killed rebuking the Delphians for
this very practice. This reference to the Delphians foreshadows the end of
Iamb 2, 192.15-17, where we hear in more detail of Aesop's fate.

because Hipponax himself has taken the role of a Cynic diatribist who complains in public about the sins of the present and augments his speeches with moralizing fables.

Hipponax's fable, the story of Bathycles' cup, begins at 191.31. Bathycles was a virtuous, old Arcadian who, on his death bed, instructed his middle son, Amphalces, to give a golden cup to the best of the Seven Wise Men. Amphalces brought it to Thales, who refused the honor and sent it to Bias. Bias in turn rejected the cup and sent it on, as did the other five. The cup was finally returned to Thales who dedicated it to Apollo (191.35-77). The original Hipponax apparently told this story in his own verse.[7]

The atmosphere of a true street diatribe is suggested by the folksy style of narration and the interruptions of the audience. The first words,

ἀνὴρ Βαθυκλῆς ᾿Αρκάς —

A man, Bathycles, an Arcadian

(191.32)

are hardly out of Hipponax's mouth before the irrepressible crowd disrupts him,

— οὐ μακρὴν ἄξω,
ὦ λῶστε μὴ σίμαινε, καὶ γὰρ οὐδ᾿ αὐτός
μέγα σχολάζ[ω·] δ[ε]ῖ με γὰρ μέσον δινεῖν
φεῦ φ]εῦ ᾿Αχέρο[ντ]ος —

I will not be long,
Oh best of men, don't snub your nose, for I
myself have not much leisure. I must whirl about
in the midst of, alas, Acheron.

(191.32-35)

Young Amphalces, the 'pre-moon' man, which is to say the Arcadian, comes 'with a favoring bird' upon Thales who is scratching a geometrical figure into the ground with his stick (191.56-58). The eminent geometer did not devise it himself, we are told, but Phrygian Euphorbus, whom Pythagoras, the sixth century mystic-mathematician, claimed was an earlier incarnation of himself (D.S. 10.6.1). Hipponax then proceeds to make fun of Pythagorean dietary habits,

---

[7] Diog. Laert. 1.28 says that Callimachus' direct source was Leandrius of Miletus. See Dawson, 23-24.

κἠδίδαξε νηστεύειν
τῶν ἐμπνεόντων· οἱ ['Ιταλοὶ ὑπήκουσαν,
οὐ πάντες, ἀλλ' οὓς εἶχεν οὕτερος δαίμων.

He taught men to refrain from living things.
The Italians obeyed, not all, but those whom
the evil daimon possessed.[8]

(191.61-63)

Those whom the evil daimon possesses are not wicked, but rather
unfortunate, "hard-up." Callimachus is saying that the Italians
became vegetarians, not all of them, but only those who had
fallen on hard times and could not afford to eat meat in any case.[9]

Finally there is a moral: men who are truly wise do not fight
for pre-eminence among themselves. The *Dieg.* applies this thought
directly to the dramatic circumstances of the poem, saying that
Hipponax advises the philologoi not to be jealous of one another
(*Dieg.* VI 5-6). If the explanation of the *Dieg.* is correct, and there
is no reason to believe that it is not, we have before us a most
ironic spectacle: the surly Hipponax, speaking on behalf of Callimachus, the most vocal participant in the Alexandrian literary
controversies, asking the other quarreling literati to kindly stop
fighting, and this in the first of his iambic poems.

One wonders why the chief mover of these quarrels is suddenly
wishing them away. Unfortunately there is not enough left of the
last part of the poem (191.78ff.) to answer this question. There is a
lacuna of 17-20 lines in *P. Oxy.* 1011 in the midst of the tale of
Bathycles' Cup. When the text resumes the subject has changed.
The narrator, presumably Hipponax,[10] is describing what someone
will say when he sees a man whom he thinks is mad:

ἀλλ' ἢν ὁρῇ τις, "οὗτος 'Αλκμέων" φήσει
καὶ "φεῦγε· βάλλει· φεῦγ'" ἐρεῖ "τὸν ἄνθρωπον."

But if someone sees, he will say, "This is Alcmeon.
Run away from the man! He strikes! Run!" [11]

(191.78-79)

---

[8] The emendation of Diodorus' text is by H. Lloyd-Jones, *CR* N.S. 17
(1967) 125-127.
[9] M. L. West, "Callimachus and the Pythagoreans," *CR* 21 (1971) 330-331.
[10] He makes his exit at 191.97.
[11] Alcmeon is the proverbial madman, Timocl. *Athen.* 6.223 C = fr.
612 K.; Plaut. *Capt.* 562; Anakreonta 8 Bgk., Pf. I 170.

These lines are similar to Horace *Sat.*1.4.33-34,[12]

Omnes hi metuunt versus, odere poetas.
"Faenum habet in cornu, longe fuge!"

All of these fear poetry and hate poets,
"He has hay on his horn! Run far away!"

The bull with hay on his horns to indicate his madness is Horace, the satirist who upsets people with his verses. Similarly, "this Alcmeon" of 191.78 might be Hipponax, the iambicist whose words are equally unwelcome. Callimachus' later portrayal of the plight of the poet thought to be mad in the thirteenth *Iamb* (203.19-21) adds weight to this interpretation.

Fractions of verses which follow contain other unpleasant images:

ὁ δ' ἐξόπισθε Κω[ρ]υκαῖος ἐγχάσκει
τὴν γλῶσσαν †ελων ὡς κύων ὅταν πίνῃ,

The Cocycian gapes from behind
moving his tongue like a dog when he drinks.

(191.82-83)

Cocycians were proverbial eavesdroppers, who overheard conversation in harbors and used the illicit information to plunder merchant ships.[13] ἐγχάσκω in old comedy implies "grinning," "scoffing," "taunting" (Ar. *V.* 721; *Ach.* 1197; *Eq.* 1313).

τὰ τράχηλα γυμνάζει

He exercises the neck,

(191.86)

may relate metaphorically to τραχηλίζω, "to wring the neck" (Pf. I. 170).

μαν]θάνοντες οὐδ' ἄλφα

Those who do not even know alpha,

(191.88)

are clearly objects of a poet's contempt. The phrase κονδύλῳ καπηλεῦσ[αι (191.89) is the most obscure of all. κόνδυλος "the knuckle" appears in Aristophanes were physical force is applied

---

[12] Pf. I 170.
[13] Dawson 19.

(Ar. V. 254, 1503; *Pax* 123; *Eq.* 411). καπηλεύω "to sell retail" is used by Hipponax (fr. IV D.³ = 79.18 W.) of vending Egyptian wine. A later connotation of the word is "selling by deception," when the seller advertises his wears as being better than they are.[14]

It is impossible to glean any connected sense from these fragments. Hipponax may be offering abuse to his audience or, in the manner of Horace's rejected satirist, he may be portraying himself as its victim.

In the conclusion, literature is again a topic of discourse,

]μοῦνος εἷλε τὰς [Μο]ύσας
]χλωρὰ σῦκα τρωγούσα[ς

He alone took up the Muses
who munched on green figs.

(191.92-93)

For Archilochus and Hipponax, munching on green figs is the same as eating animal or slaves' fodder.[15] Someone is described as taking up poetry, very likely iambic poetry with its inelegant and poverty-stricken Muses. The word γέλωτος in the next line may belong to this image.

In the final lines we hear something about Charon and "the time to sail back" (191.97). We can only assume that Hipponax is speaking here of his return to Hades and that he has remained the narrator throughout. Pfeiffer estimates that there are no more than 17 lines missing after this point in the papyrus, and we may conjecture that Hipponax's speech and the first *Iambus* came to a close together.

In sum then, the first *Iamb* is a species of cynic diatribe delivered by the ghost of Hipponax to a learned audience of philologoi who are urged to stop wrangling with each other. In view of the pugnacious personality of the historical Hipponax, and the ridiculous goings on that surround the event, it is clear that the first *Iamb* is a parody of a contemporary literary phenomenon, the cynic diatribe, as well as a statement about Callimachus' literary model, Hipponactean choliambs. The subject of literature surfaces from time to time in the poem, but there are preserved no complete lines which reveal 'Hipponax's' point of view on the subject.

---

[14] W. S. Barrett, *Hippolytus* (Oxford 1964) 344 where he cites Plat. *Prt.* 313C-E.
[15] Hipponax fr. 39.5-6 D.³ = 26.5-6 W.; Eustathius *Od.* 1828.11.

Iamb 2 (fr. 192)

The second *Iamb* follows easily from the first. It is an animal fable, written in stichic choliambi and narrated by another Ionian, Aesop of Sardis:

ταῦτα δ' Αἴσωπος
ὁ Σαρδιηνὸς εἶπεν, ὅντιν' οἱ Δελφοί
ᾄδοντα μῦθον οὐ καλῶς ἐδέξαντο.

These things, Aesop the Sardinian said,
whom the Delphians did not receive kindly
when he was telling the tale.

(192.15-17)

That the Delphians did not receive Aesop well is an understatement. The story of his experiences at Delphi is alluded to in 191.27 and is briefly narrated by the scholia in reference to that line. Aesop rebuked the Delphians for living off the sacrifices, and for his efforts he was thrown over a cliff or stoned to death (Schol. Flor. 20-26). At 191.27 the ghost of Hipponax likens his audience to greedy Delphians. At the conclusion to *Iamb* 2, the Delphians are seen to be Aesop's audience also, and the cause of Aesop's death. The experience of Aesop is an example of the reception archetypically accorded to a fabulist who has come to educate his audience.[16] Callimachus invites us to see himself in the same tradition.

Like the fable of Bathycles' Cup, Aesop's tale begins in an unadorned, homespun fashion,

Ἦν κεῖνος οὑνιαυτός, ᾧ τό τε πτηνόν
καὶ τοὐν θαλάσσῃ καὶ τὸ τετράπουν αὕτως
ἐφθέγγεθ' ὡς ὁ πηλὸς ὁ Προμήθειος

It was that time when the winged tribe
and the one in the sea and the four-footed one
spoke just like Promethean clay.[17]

(192.1-3)

---

[16] The historical Hipponax also seems to have portrayed himself as the victim of stoning 32 D.³ = 37 W.

[17] Classification of animals by their means of locomotion is standard procedure throughout fifth century literature, and afterwards in Plato (*Phd.* 250E; *Smp.* 207A) and Aristotle (*PA* 697ᵇ23; *HA* 488A). Callimachus manages to vary these expressions by using a prepositional phrase to describe the central group, and adjectives for the first and third.

Our text breaks off, but according to the *Dieg.* the animals perpe-
trated acts of defiance against the gods. "They spoke in the same
voice as men until the swan negotiated with the gods on the matter
of eliminating old age, and the fox dared to say that Zeus did not
rule justly" (*Dieg.* VI 23-27). The meager remnants of lines 4-6
are all that remains of the section thus summarized.[18] The *Dieg.*
continues, "Then he transferred their voice into men, and they
became talkative" (*Dieg.* VI 27-29). This is clearly a summary of
lines 7-10 of the text, of which Pfeiffer says rightly, "res ipsa a
Dieg. satis certa, at sententiarum structura et nexus adhuc
obscura."[19]

The second *Iamb*, then, appears at first to be a not untypical
animal fable.[20] Callimachus, however, includes several more details
which give the story a novel and allegorical interpretation.
"Eudemos," he says, "has the voice of a dog; Philton, of an ass;
someone else (lacuna) of a parrot; and the tragedians, have the
voice of those living in the sea" (192.10-13). His mentioning the
tragedians as a group leaves no doubt that he is indulging himself
here in a bit of literary polemic.

Eudemos and Philton are unknown. Since Hellenistic writers
do not criticize each other by name, it seems likely that Philton
and Eudemos are not the personal names of Callimachus' rivals.
It is not obvious why Callimachus chose to use these particular
names here.[21] Since the *Dieg.* mentions only these two specific

---

[18] In line 4 someone is speaking of the times of Kronos and eras even
before that when things were, presumably, better. λ. .ουσα in line 5 suggests
a feminine speaker, perhaps the fox. Line 6 reflects the fox's argument,
but it seems to be part of a third person narrative. In any case, the animals'
accusations appear to end here.

[19] Pf. I 173. The sentence is interrupted by a parenthesis which only adds
to the difficulty (192.8-9). Pfeiffer translates "quasi non nobis ipsis vim
habentibus etiam ceteris partem dedicandi" and interprets, "Juppiter
animalium quidem ademit vocem, transtulit autem in hominum genus iam
per se loquacissimum." This is the most popular interpretation, as it follows
the *Dieg.* (See also Dawson 29; Trypanis 115.)

[20] E.g. 383 Halm = 240 Perry.

[21] There was a well-known Eudemos, a fifth century Athenian druggist,
who frequently appeared in Attic comedy as a dispenser of amulets and
poisons (Ar. *Pl.* 883). It may be that Callimachus is here using a traditional
comic figure to present the character of the man he is insulting, as Horace
(*Sat.* 2.8) describes a dinner at which there are characters with stock comic
names such as Porcius who eats like a pig, and Balatro, a buffoon.
On the other hand Eudemos could be the real name of an acquaintance

names (VI 29-30), it is generally assumed that the possessor(s) of the parrot's voice should be the name of a group of writers, which would parallel *tragodoi*. Several scholars have suggested rhetoricians.[22]

As Hipponax in the first *Iamb* insults the philologoi by likening them to wasps and flies, so here Callimachus berates these artists by likening their voices to those of a dog, an ass, a parrot, and fish. His choice of animals is not particularly imaginative. The dog appears as a term of reproach in 191.83. In the first book of the *Aitia* (1.30-34) Callimachus specifically denigrates the braying of the ass and opposes it to the clear voice of the cicada with which he identifies his own singing. The parrot is an obvious tag with which to label a literary rival since this bird mindlessly repeats what it has heard. The parrot also exemplifies the fable's original premise, that animals could once talk like men. The voice of the fish is more puzzling. Pfeiffer, in his notes remarks, "pisces non muti fuerant," and refers to Babrius, *Prooem.* 1.10,

ἐλάλει δὲ κίχθύς

and the fish prattled.

Platt prefers to think that "those who dwell in the sea" are sea-gulls.[23] The image, in any case, is not very flattering.

The conclusion summarizes the poet's view.

οἱ δὲ πάντες [ἄνθρωποι
καὶ πουλύμυθοι καὶ λάλοι πεφ[ύκασιν

All men are
verbose and over-wordy.[24]

(192.13-14)

One thinks of Horace's words on Lucilius,

At dixi fluere hunc lutulentum, saepe ferentem
plura quidem tollenda relinquendis.

---

of the poet. There was a physician of that name at the court of Ptolemy I (Gal. 15.134) as well as a peripatetic called Eudemos of Rhodes who may have been associated with Praxiphanes, one of the Telchines of the *Aitia* prologue. Callimachus' *Epigram* 47 also mentions a Eudemos.

[22] Pf. I 173; Puelma 224, n. 1.

[23] A. Platt, "Callimachus *Iambi* 162-170," *CQ* 4 (1910) 205.

[24] As Euhemerus in 191.11.

> But I said that he flows muddy, often carrying
> more that ought to be removed than left behind.
>
> *(Sat.* 1.10.50-51)

πάντες in 192.13 suggests that the criticism is meant to have a wide application, perhaps beyond those individuals and groups he specifically mentions. The poem ends with the surprise revelation that the narrator is Aesop (192.15-17 discussed above).

Iambi 1 and 2, then, are intimately related. Meter, dialect and tone are the same. The first is a harangue with a fable inserted, the second, a fable alone. Both look back upon an earlier time when moral standards were high and decry the behavior of the present i.e. of their audience. As far as we can tell from our present text, the first touches but does not dwell upon literary issues, the second makes the over-wordiness of present-day authors its central point. Both poems are narrated by a persona. The first is put into the mouth of Hipponax, who belongs to the Ionic tradition of iambic verse, and the second is told by Aesop, who represents a more popular and prosaic kind of moralizing literature. These two literary strains, together with the Cynic diatribe, which is parodied in *Iamb* 1, are some of the various literary components from which Callimachus forges his own recreation of the iambic genre.

Iamb 3 (fr. 193)

At its outset, the third *Iamb* poses as a typical Hellenistic moralizing choliambic poem against *aischrokerdeia*,[25] in close alliance with *Iambi* 1 and 2. The *Dieg.* (VI 34-37) tells us specifically that Callimachus accuses the present age of being concerned with wealth rather than with *arete*, and that he prefers the previous epoch which embraced the opposite values. This seems to be the subject of lines 1-18, as far as we can judge from the ruins of the papyrus. Only the final portions of these lines are extant, and it is possible to identify only a few general themes which are common in this kind of poetry. The *Dieg.* mentions the topic of wealth placed above morality (VI 34-35). On the other side of the coin, the poet laments his own poverty in lines 15-17. Line 10,

ληκῆσαι

---

[25] For examples see Chapt. 3, pp. 66-67 below.

indicates that Callimachus is also concerned with sexual abuses,[26] while lines 13 and 14,

α]ἰ κακαὶ ψῆφοι
ἀνάσσ[ο]ντε[ς

seem to deal with political corruption.[27]

After its summary of the moralistic part of the poem, the *Dieg.* (VI 37-40) asserts that Callimachus incidentally attacked a certain Euthydemos because he had been introduced to a rich man by his mother and was using up his youth for profit. We first meet Euthydemos at line 24 where his mother is portrayed as doing, or having done, something to her son. In 25 Callimachus complains,

νῦν οὐδὲ πῦρ ἐναύουσιν

Now they do not even kindle fire.

The plural subject is probably the boy and his mother. Denial of so basic a right as kindling fire is an expression of social ostracism, so it appears that these two are no longer talking to the poet.

The cause of their attitude was apparently explained in lines 26-33 which seem to describe a meeting between Euthydemos and the poet. The details are not very clear, and theories abound about the nature of their encounter. Tsiribas and Coppola have proposed that it involves the making and breaking of a marriage contract,[28] which does not seem justified by the fragments. Dawson maintains more reasonably that the pledge which they had made was of homosexual love.[29] Euthydemos is probably not the name of an actual lover of the poet's, but an archetype for a youthful lover on the Socratic model.[30]

---

[26] Dawson 35 n. 10 gives a long and convincing argument which shows that ληκῆσαι ought to be derived not from ληκέω as LSJ asserts, but rather from ληκάω == λαικάζω.

[27] Perhaps after the example of Hesiod railing at injustice, e.g. *Op.* 256-262.

[28] D. A. Tsiribas, "Καλλιμάχου Ἴαμβος κατὰ Εὐθυδήμου," *Athena* 59 (1955) 162.

[29] C. Dawson, "An Alexandrian Prototype of Marathus?" *AJP* 67 (1946) 7.

[30] There was a famous Euthydemos called ὁ καλός a devoted follower of Socrates with whom the wealthy and aristocratic Critias fell in love (Pl. *Symp.* 222B; Xen. *Mem.* 1.2.29 and 4.2.1-6). According to Xenophon's account, Socrates tried strenuously to dissuade Critias from making sexual overtures to the boy, and when Critias refused to be moved, Socrates insulted him by likening his social habits to those of a pig (Xen. *Mem.* 1.2.29-31).

Whatever the nature of the pledge made between them at the meeting, the poet clearly expresses his sense of being wronged by Euthydemos subsequently,

]χρηγύως ἐπαιδεύθην
ἐ]φρόνησα τὠγαθὸν βλέψαι

I was educated rightly.
I thought I saw the good.

(193.30-31)

He wishes he had never become involved with the boy at all, claiming extravagantly that he would have been better off had he been a eunuch devotee of Cybele or of Adonis (193.34-38), rather than what he is now, "mad," μάργος because he "nodded" to the Muses, that is, because he is a poet (193.38-39). The remains of the final line of the poem are unclear (193.39), but Dawson cannot be far wrong in associating it with the proverb, ἤν τις ἔμαξε μᾶζαν, ταύτην καὶ ἐσθιέτω "I have kneaded my bread, now I must eat it." [31] If μάργος is given the meaning 'gluttonous,' the proverb is especially appropriate.

Callimachus sees his art as being primarily responsible for his failure with Euthydemos. His art leads to poverty, and poverty to rejection. His frustration over Euthydemos' preference for material wealth over song is expressed in the attack against *ai-schrokerdeia* which introduces the poem. He quickly lapses from this lofty moralizing to dramatizing the intimate details of a painful and seemingly personal experience in Alexandrian society, where others did not always set as high a value on the poet's achievement as he did himself.

In *Iamb* 3 Callimachus uses the form of contemporary moralizing literature in a unique way. Fables give way to current events, and all of the moralizing on the corrupting power of wealth in the opening lines is motivated less by high-mindedness than by the fact that the poet's sex life is being ruined by lack of money. Unlike 1 and 2, the narrative of 3 is presented in the first person which gives the impression that the poet is talking about his own experiences and feelings. This intimate tone is entirely new and breaks the illusion of the poet-diatribist completely. It is nearest in feeling to the Latin love elegy.[32]

---

[31] Dawson 37.
[32] See chapt. 4 below.

Iamb 4 (fr. 194)

Iamb 4 has many close connections to the first three. It is written
in stichic choliambs and Ionian dialect, and it has at its heart
a fable about the evils of strife which is set in a contemporary
framework. The remains include two continuous passages containing 63 lines and 14 lines, linked together by a bridge of 8 half-lines,
plus assorted fragments and the outline provided by the *Dieg*.
It is possible in *Iamb* 4, more than in any other, to see in detail
the intricacies of Callimachus' art.

The *Dieg.* supplies the setting for the poem. A certain Simos
interrupts a quarrel between the poet and an unnamed rival.
Each of the combatants must have been insisting on their own
superiority, for Simos attempts to conclude the argument by
asserting that he himself is the equal of both (*Dieg.* VII 2-5).
Callimachus subjects the interloper to a round of abuse, calling
him Θρᾶχα and παιδοκλέπτης (*Dieg.* VII 5-6),[33] terms which suit
the name Simos.[34] Simos must be the son of Charitades rejected
by the poet on line 1 of the text itself, and the insults must have
been in the lost lines 194.2-5, for at line 6, Callimachus has already
begun to tell a tale of a proverbial quarrel on Mt. Tmolus between
a laurel and an olive tree who were interrupted by a thorny bramble
bush.[35] The fable is obviously intended to instruct Simos.

Like the story of Bathycles' Cup, it begins with an admonition
to listen, followed by a typical folksy introduction,

ἄκουε δὴ τὸν αἶνον· ἔν κοτε Τμώλῳ
δάφνην ἐλαίη νεῖχος οἱ πάλαι Λυδοί
λέγουσι θέσθαι

Listen to the story. Once on Tmolus
the ancient Lydians say,
the laurel tree quarreled with the olive.

(194.6-8)

[33] The Thracian poets Orpheus and Thamyris are both reputed to have
invented pederasty. Eubul. fr. 75.3 K. quoted by Pf. I, 177. See also M.
Pohlenz "Der römer Gaius bei Kallimachos," *Philologus* 90 (1935) 121 n. 3.
[34] Pf. I, 177. In *Iamb* 1 Hipponax silences a heckler saying,

. . . μὴ σίμαινε,

Don't turn up your nose.
(191.33)
i.e. "Don't be a Simos." Simos is the "snub-nosed," a trait associated by
the Greeks with thievery and lechery.
[35] Dawson (52) points out that the story line is a traditional one, e.g.
Aesop Fab. 385 Halm.

In the style of Aesopic fables, narration is kept to a minimum throughout and the dramatic situation is developed through the speeches of the participants.

The laurel is already concluding the exordium of her principal speech with an unkind remark about the color of the olive's leaves when continuous text begins on line 22.[36] Combining narratio and confirmatio she begins a formal presentation of her own best qualities in three subject areas each clearly marked by a direct address to her opponent. In each of the three areas the laurel makes three points. She begins by boasting of three religious associations. Two are expressed in three rhetorical questions and the third in an emphatic statement: What house does she not adorn by the doorpost? (194.24); What seer does not employ her? What sacrificer? (194.25); the Pythia sits on laurel, sings of laurel and makes her bed of laurel (194.26-27).

A brief address to the olive (194.28) punctuates the transition to topic two, her special ties to Apollo. A reminder of how Branchus used a laurel branch to heal the sons of the Ionians (194.28-30) serves as an introduction to her three associations with Apolline ritual: She participates in the Athenian procession of the Pythaistai (194.32-33); she is the prize at the Pythian games (194.33); and she plays a key role in the Daphnephoria (194.34-36).

At line 37 she changes the subject again, marking the change as before with a direct address to the olive (194.37).[37] Her grand peroratio follows, an overblown boast of her ritual purity which she contrasts with the disgrace of the olive's traditional associations with funeral ceremonies (194.37-43).

The olive answers the laurel's arguments with equal rhetorical finesse. She begins dramatically with an ironical exclamatio,

ὦ πάντα καλή,

Oh beautiful in every way!

(194.46)

which contrasts with and mocks the laurel's

ὤφρων ἐλαίη

Oh senseless olive!

(194.28; 37)

---

[36] The laurel likens the two-tone coloration of the olive to that of a snake's belly, on one hand, and to a slave's sunburnt skin on the other (194.22-23). This interpretation was first suggested by G. Murray in *P. Oxy.* 1011, 75.

[37] ὤφρων ἐλαία as in line 18 and 28.

She follows with a confutatio in which she answers the laurel's arguments in reverse order, beginning with her role in the funeral ritual,

τῶν ἐμῶν τὸ κ[άλλιστον
ἐν τῇ τελευτῇ κύκνος [ὡς ᾿Απόλλωνος
ἤεισας·

The most beautiful of my associations
at the end, like the swan of Apollo,
you have sung.

(194.46-48)

She gives three examples of those whom she proudly escorts to the grave: the young men whom Ares has slain (194.49); and the old, a Tethys or Tithonus (194.52-53). The honor of burying the dead gives her more pleasure than the laurel could possibly feel when she is escorted from Tempe in the Daphnephoria (194. 55-56). Since the laurel brought up the subject, the olive is the prize at the Olympic games which are greater than the Pythian (194.56-59).

The olive abruptly interrupts her confutatio at this point to introduce some new subject areas. She makes the arguments obliquely, quoting two crows whom she pretends to hear chattering in her leaves (194.59-63). The birds pose as referees in a wrestling match between the trees. The three falls which determine victory in wrestling are matched by three topics which the birds consider: Who discovered each of the trees? (194.64-68); Which of the gods honors each? (194.69-72); Of what use is their fruit? (194.73-78). Since the crows call a draw at issue two (who can judge between Apollo and Athena?) a fourth question is necessary to determine the victor: Whose branch do suppliants hold? (194.79). The conclusion is swift,

τὰ τρί᾽ ἡ δάφνη κεῖται.

The laurel takes three falls.[38]

(194.80)

The dramatic conceit is concluded by an aside (194.81-82) and the olive begins again where she left off, answering the laurel's

---

[38] The wrestling motif was perhaps borrowed from Aristophanes' *Frogs* 1269 and 1272 where Dionysus similarly referees the contest between Aeschylus and Euripides.

arguments. This part of the text is badly damaged. It is clear, however, that the olive mentions both seers (194.90) and the doorpost (194.91) and that she concludes on line 93, ending where the laurel began.

The trees organize their arguments with a view toward symmetry and *varietas* is the best manner of professional rhetoricians. They both favor the number three in arranging their arguments and examples, with the second or third element different in some small way from the others. Their phrasing has equal polish, as the following examples will show.

The laurel presents two of her general religious associations with three rhetorical questions, introduced almost identically (repetitio),

> τίς δ' οἶκος οὗπερ [ο]ὐκ ἐγὼ παρὰ φλιῇ;
> τίς δ' οὔ με μάντις ἢ τίς οὐ θύτης ἕλκει;
>
> (194.24-25)

She emphasizes the three ways in which the Pythia uses laurel with unsubtle repetitions of her own name (conduplicatio),

> καὶ Πυθίη γὰρ ἐν δάφνῃ μὲν ἵδρυται,
> δάφνην δ' ἀείδει καὶ δάφνην ὑπέστρωται.
>
> (194.26-27)

She frequently repeats herself using synonyms e.g.

> ...οὐχὶ γινώσκω
> οὐδ' οἶδ'...
>
> (194.37-38)

and

> ἁγνὴ γάρ εἰμι, ...
> ἱρὴ γάρ εἰμι·
>
> (194.39-40)

The olive and her co-conspirators, the crows, are not to be undone. Their own questions appear in parallel order,

> τίς δ' εὗρε δάφνην; ...
> ὡς πρῖνον, ὡς δρῦν, ὡς κύπειρον, ὡς πεύκην.
> τίς δ' εὗρ' ἐλαίην; ...
>
> (194.64-66),

and also in chiastic order,

τίς τὴν ἐλαίην, τίς δὲ [τ]ὴν δάφνην τιμᾷ;
δάφνην Ἀπόλλων, ἡ δὲ Παλλὰς ἦν εὖρε.

(194.70-71)

In spite of the formality of their arguments, the trees have lively and well-developed personalities. The olive is sophisticated and ironic. She calls the laurel πάντα καλή (194.46) and lightly turns the laurel's worst insult into her own greatest pride (194.46-54).

The laurel, in contrast, has the angry temper of an iambicist. She attacks both of her opponents directly, calling the olive a slave (194.22-23); charging her with unseemly acts (194.40-43), repeating the insulting ὤφρων ἐλαίη (194.18,28,37); and swearing at the bramble (194.103-106). She also has a tendency toward self-dramatization which is revealed in her diction. She is given to coining Aeschylean compounds such as ἡλιοπλήξ (194.23) and οὐλαφηφόρος (194.38), and to imitating tragic phrasing as in

τίς δ' οἶκος οὗπερ [ο]ὐκ ἐγὼ παρὰ φλιῇ;

(194.24).[39]

The presumptuous bramble tries to compete with her,

οὐκ ὦ τάλαιναι παυσόμεσθα, μὴ χαρταί
γενώμεθ' ἐχθροῖς,

Shall we not cease, oh wretches, lest
we become joys to our enemies? [40]

(194.98-99)

The laurel makes a ludicrously suitable response,

τὴν δ' ἄρ' ὑποδρὰξ οἷα ταῦρος ἡ δάφνη
ἔβλεψε...

Like a bull, the laurel looked at her askance,[41]

(194.101-102)

and the words that follow are worthy of Hipponax himself,

ὦ κακὴ λώβη,
ὡς δὴ μἰ' ἡμέων καὶ σύ; μή με ποιῆσαι
Ζεὺς τοῦτο· καὶ γὰρ γειτονεῦσ' ἀποπνίγεις

---

[39] Sophocles fr. 942 P. (Pf. I, 179).
[40] A. Pers. 1034.
[41] Like Euripides Med. 92 and 188. Ar. Ra. 804. (Pf. I, 183).

Oh pernicious outrage,
One of us? You? May Zeus forbid it!
When you are near you suffocate me!

(194.102-104)

Line 103 recalls the first line of the poem,

Εἶς — οὐ γάρ; — ἡμέων, παῖ Χαριτάδεω, καὶ σύ

You too, one of us? Isn't that what you mean,
Son of Charitades?

(194.1) [42]

indicating that the bramble is to be equated with the son of Charitades who is excluded from a group in line 1 and who is presumably
the Simos mentioned by the *Dieg.*

The similarity between the situation of the trees and that of the
poet and his acquaintances as it is described by the *Dieg.* seems
like an invitation to give the fable an allegorical interpretation.
A. D. Knox was the first to take this view. Knox sees Callimachus
as the laurel, Herodas as the olive, and their argument as contemporary literary debate about metrics.[43] Puelma prefers to identify
the olive as Callimachus because she is a victim, which is a role
Callimachus likes to play and because she has a sophisticated
style. Puelma also believes that the bramble is Callimachus because
he takes the peace-making role Callimachus-Hipponax plays in
Iamb 1. Callimachus' playing a double role should be understood
as a typical Hellenistic subtlety.[44]

The differences in these interpretations cannot be resolved by
searching the text for subtle references to hidden agendas in an
Alexandrian literary debate. There are none to be found. The
details of the poem support neither Knox's not Puelma's allegories.
The links between Callimachus' relationships with his two friends
and the three trees on Mt. Tmolus is better understood in terms
of the nature of the genre itself and Callimachus' exploitation of it.

Fables are intended to instruct their listeners by implying that
there are analogies between the characters in the story and the
listeners themselves. In *Iamb* 1 e.g. the audience of philologoi

---

[42] Quoted by the *Dieg.* VII 1 but lost from the principal papyrus which
cannot be read before line 6, *P. Oxy.* 1011 fol. 4ʳ 17-28.
[43] A. D. Knox, "Herodes and Callimachus," *Philologus* 81 (1925-26)
253-254.
[44] Puelma 237-247.

is supposed to compare itself, to its own disadvantage, with the seven wise men. In *Iamb* 4 the bramble represents the son of Charitades, whom the *Dieg.* calls Simos, and Callimachus and his rival are the laurel and the olive. The moral would seem to be that the son of Charitades is as inferior to Callimachus and his friend as the bramble is to a laurel or an olive.

If the moral is stated explicitly anywhere in the poem, it is in the lost section at the end. In the considerable extant remains the bramble has but one sentence to speak (194.98-100) and very little importance. It is clear, in spite of the tattered text, that the poet has put his major emphasis on the elegantly contrived debate between the laurel and the olive, and that there, if anywhere, lies the meaning of the fourth *Iamb*.

The centrality of the debate is directly related to the nature of the genre itself. Fables, which are essentially metaphors in the form of a narrative, have a rhetorical nature even in their most primitive form,[45] and often contain simple rhetorical devices such as direct address and parentheses. In *Iamb* 4 Callimachus exaggerates the rhetorical nature of the fable by presenting it in the form of a debate elaborately constructed in the fashion of professional rhetoricians. In this way Callimachus both acknowledges the true nature of the genre and comically burlesques it.

While illuminating the nature of the genre, the arboreal rhetoricians also parody human rhetoricians and the verbal tricks of their trade. The exaggerated characteristics of the iambicist laurel and sophisticated olive can also be understood as parodies of certain contemporary literary types. The parody is accomplished in the traditional way by separating form from content, by making the master of oratorical finesse, the solemn enunciator of tragic phrases, dispenser of Hipponactean scorn and arbiter elegantarum trees. That the literary attitudes here being parodied include several that Callimachus himself often assumes only increases our admiration for this witty tour de force.

Iamb 5 (fr. 195)

Iamb 5 is a transition poem. It is the first of the epodes, and the last of the diatribes. Its meter combines a line of choliambic

---

[45] For discussion see *Babrius and Phaedrus*, B. E. Perry (ed. and trans.), Loeb Classical Library (Cambridge Mass. 1965) xix-xxiv.

trimeters, used in the previous poems, with a line of plain iambic dimeters which will appear in several poems following.

Like 1-4, it contains an attack on moral corruption, which, as in Iamb 3, is placed in a contemporary setting. The *Dieg.* tells us that the poet is speaking to a schoolmaster "with the intention to be useful," accusing the schoolmaster of sexual abuses against his pupils,[46]

ἰαμβίζει ὡς
τοὺς ἰδίους μαθητὰς καταισχύνον-
τα, ἐν ἤθει εὐνοίας ἀπαγ[ο]ρεύων τού-
τῳ δρᾶν, μὴ ἀλῷ.

(*Dieg.* VII 21-24)

J. Stroux has shown that καταισχύνειν refers specifically to homosexual behavior,[47] sometimes in the context of a pupil-teacher relationship.[48] The obscene sense may also be extended to include δρᾶν (*Dieg.* VII 24), which, Stroux asserts, ought to be understood as a substitute for the Attic πράττειν,[49] itself a well-attested example of homosexual jargon. The allegorical interpretation of the *Dieg.* is supported by Choeroboscus, who claims that Callimachus uses allegory in lines 23 and following because he was ashamed to say what he wished.[50]

The poem begins this way:

Ὦ ξεῖνε — συμβουλὴ γὰρ ἕν τι τῶν ἱρῶν —
ἄκουε τἀπὸ καρδ[ίης,
ἐπεί σε δαίμων ἄλφα βῆτ[α

Oh stranger, for advice is something sacred,
listen to some heartfelt words.
Since the daimon (has made you a teacher of) the alphabet,

(195.1-3).

---

[46] Dawson 63 points out that it is not altogether clear just whose pupils were abused. "The word ἰδίους in the *Diegesis* may have been used clumsily to refer to the pupils of Callimachus."

[47] J. Stroux, "Erzahlungen aus Kallimachos," *Ph.* 89 (1934) 317.

[48] Lucian *D. Metretr.* 10.

[49] Stroux, above n. 47, 317, Archil. 72 D.³ = 119 W. δρήστης "a sexual doer." Dawson 57, n. 24 points out that δρᾶν can also refer to the common formula ἀλλὰ πιθοῦ μηδ' ἄλλως ποιεῖ.

[50] In Spengel *Rh. Gr.* III 245. quoted by Pf. I 186.

W. Bühler, has compared these lines to Hipponax's X D.³ = 118 W.,[51]

ὦ Σάνν', ἐπειδὴ ῥῖνα θεό[συλιν φύ]εις,
    καὶ γαστρὸς οὐ κατακρα[τεῖς,
λαιμᾶι δέ σοι τὸ χεῖλος ὡς ἐρωιδιοῦ
[   ]
τούς μοι παράσχες [
    σύν τοί τι βουλεῦσαι θέ[λω.

Oh Sannos, since you grow a sacrilegious nose
and have no control over your stomach,
your lip is hungry like the beak of a heron,

Lend me your ear . . .
I wish to give some advice to you.

(X D.³ = 118.1-6 W.)

Bühler makes the following observations: both iambi are addressed directly to the enemy; both begin with an apostrophe; both contain an ἐπεί clause justifying the poet's outburst; in both cases the poet claims to give advice; and the opponent is admonished to listen; in neither case is the poet's true intention to be of help, but rather to abuse the addressee.

The structure of Callimachus' opening, then, and his topos are adapted from Hipponax. The substance of Callimachus' attack however is very different. Beginning at line 23, the poet offers the teacher two kinds of advice. First he admonishes him to put out a fire,

τὸ πῦρ δὲ τὠνέκαυσας, ἄχρις οὐ πολλῆ
    πρόσω κεχώρηκεν φλογί,
ἀλλ' ἀτρεμίζει κἠπὶ τὴν τέφρην οἴ[χ]νεῖ,
    κοίμησον.

The fire which you kindled, as long as the flame
has not gone much forward,
but is quiet and goes over the ash,
put it to bed.

(195.23-26)

Taking a clue from the *Dieg.*, most commentators interpret this passage as a warning to the schoolmaster to quench his erotic

⁵¹ W. Bühler, "Archilochos und Kallimachos" in *Archiloque*, Fond. Hardt Entretiens 10 (Genève 1963) 225-247.

desires. Fire is a traditional metaphor for burning, all-consuming
love. Both Dawson and Pfeiffer offer many examples of this usage
from contemporary Hellenistic literature.[52] Lucilius and Horace
use it both heterosexual and homosexual relationships.[53]

In his second piece of advice, the poet suddenly changes his
metaphor, but the meaning is the same, he is cautioning the
schoolmaster to tame his runaway libido,

> ἴσχε δὲ δρόμου
> μαργῶντας ἵππους μηδὲ δευτέρην κάμψῃς,
>   μή τοι περὶ νύσσῃ δίφρον
> ἄξωσιν, ἐκ δὲ κύμβαχος κυβιστήσῃς.

Hold back from the course the mad horses,
and do not guide them round a second time,
lest they wreck the car around the turning post
and you tumble headlong out.

(195.26-29)

This metaphor too is a commonplace.[54]

Finally the poet indicates that neither he nor his advice is
understood. He urges the schoolmaster to work out the puzzle,

> ἐγὼ Βάκις τοι καὶ Σίβυλλα [καὶ] δάφνη
>   καὶ φηγός. ἀλλὰ συμβαλεῦ
> τὠνιγμα, καὶ μὴ Πιτθέως ἔχε χρείην·

I am your Bakis and Sibyl and laurel
and oak. Solve the riddle
and do not have need for Pittheus.

(195.31-33)

Pittheos is an interpreter of oracles (Eur. *Med* 675-86). The poem
has 33 more lines which cannot be read.

The fifth *Iamb*, then, is Hipponactean invective with an unexpected twist. The target of the abuse does not understand a
single word of it. This fact, probably not obvious before line 31,
makes the invective absurd, for what can its power be if it eludes
its intended victim? As the absurd content of the arboreal debate
in *Iamb* 4 turns elaborate rhetorical devices into a parody of

---

[52] Pf. I 186; Dawson 59 nts. 23-25.
[53] Lucilius 74 M.; Horace *Epode* 11.4.
[54] Anacreon's verses on the Thracian filly (88 D.³) are a striking example
of the use of this metaphor in earlier Greek lyric.

rhetoric, so here, incomprehensible insults make a parody of Hipponactean invective, which is nothing if not straightforward. In the place of obscene insult Callimachus puts a riddle, τὤνιγμα, in the manner of Lycophron's *Alexandra*. In fact, when Callimachus claims to be oracular, a Bakis, Sibyl, laurel and oak, he seems very like Cassandra,

Κλάρου Μιμαλλών, ἢ Μελαγκραίρας κόπις
Νησοῦς θυγατρός, ἤ τι Φίκιον τέρας,

a frenzied prophetess (Mimallon of Claros),
or Sibyl (babbler of Melancraera, Neso's daughter),
or Sphinx (Phician monster).

(*Alexandra* 1464-65)

Riddles appear early in Greek popular literature where they are often found as oracles or as capping lines in verse contests. When elaborated, they become fables or *ainoi*. The collection of riddles made by Clearchus of Soli (fr. 61-68 FHG) attests to the scholarly interest they generated in the time of Callimachus, and Lycophron's *Alexandra*, the literary interest. As Callimachus incorporates fables into Hipponactean invective in *Iambi* 1 and 2, so in 5 he does the same with riddles. The effect of separating invective from its normal contexts and riddles from their usual environment is to jolt the reader into looking anew at both. The result is a radically different kind of iambic poetry in which literary forms are as tortured and ridiculed as a Bupalus or Lykambes.

Iamb 6 (fr. 196)

The metrical change in *Iamb* 5 anticipates a development in the *Iambi* that begins in earnest with *Iamb* 6, the first of the non-choliambic, non-Ionic, non-Hipponactean *Iambi*. As in the fifth, the metrical system is epodic, this time combining iambic trimeter and ithyphallic. Its dialect is Doric and its direct literary sources are unknown.

Like poems 1-5 the sixth is addressed to a single individual with whom the author, or at least his persona, is ostensibly acquainted (*Dieg.* VII 25-26); but here, according to the *Dieg.*, the poet tells no story, but describes the length, height, and width of the base, throne, and footstool of the statue of Zeus at Olympia, which his friend was sailing off to see (*Dieg.* VII 25-29).

Iamb 6 then is a kind of *propemptikon* in the form of an elaborate *ekphrasis*.[55] Its meaning has largely eluded the poem's commentators. Most critics tend to regard the work as a tableau on which Callimachus displays his learning, revealing himself to be the ultimate *poeta doctus*. Dawson (72) sums up this view as well as any, "The poet indulged in a *tour de force*, putting into verse some paragraphs from an ancient Baedeker; displaying τέχνη rather than ἐνθουσιασμός and admirably illustrating the criticism of Ovid (*Am* 1.15.14), quamvis ingenio non valet, arte valet."

The text, such as we have it, seems to bear Dawson out. Callimachus begins by focusing on the artist himself,

'Αλεῖος ὁ Ζεύς, ἁ τέχνα δὲ Φειδία

Zeus of Elis, the art of Phidias

(196.1).

The technical description of the statue begins at line 23,

καὶ τὠπίβαθρον τῶ θρόν[ω] τὸ χρύ[σι]ον
    . . . ἐπλάτυνται.
    . . . πέντε τε[τ]ρ[άκι]ν [πο]δῶν

and the golden base of the throne
is wide.
20 feet.

(196.23-25)

These lines are unusually full, and serve as a good example of the descriptive verses which apparently continue in this manner until line 44. They seem to consist largely of quite prosaic numerical measurements and are poetical in neither diction nor subject matter. Although Callimachus deliberately uses the language of a true *demiourgos*, he accomplishes the task with customary finesse. He employs a truly impressive variety of measuring standards,[56] and new adjectives and nouns appear here and there.[57]

---

[55] Detailed descriptions of works of art appear regularly in Greek literature as early as Homer and Hesiod. They were especially popular in Hellenistic literature e.g. Apollonius' description of Jason's cloak 1.721 ff. and Theocritus' description of the cup in *Id.* 1.27 ff.

[56] πούς (196.25); τετράδωρον (196.27); παλαστή (196.28); πᾶχυς (196.38); ὄργυια (196.43).
For information on the controversy over the actual measurements of the statue see Pf. I 189.

[57] Λυδιεργὲς (196.29); ἐφεδρίδος (196.37).

In a rare complete sentence at line 37, he speaks of the figure of Zeus itself,

αὐτὸς δ' ὁ δαίμων πέντ[ε] τ[ᾶ]ς ἐφεδρ[ί]δος
παχέεσσι μάσσων·

The god himself is five cubits greater than the seat.

(196.37-38)

The Nike of line 39 must be the one which Pausanias (5.2.1) describes as being in Zeus' right hand. The Horae (196.42) Pausanias (5.2.7) says were on the highest point of the throne, above the head of the statue with a similar group of Charites, who must be the fathom-high maidens of line 43.

The *Aitia* (fr. 114) contains a similar though much briefer description of the statue of Delian Apollo.[58] It presents information on the height, material and general appearance of the statue: it was 18 cubits high, made of gold, nude, and carried a bow in its right hand, a group of Charites in its left. The passage takes the form of a dialogue between the statue itself and a passerby in the style of certain epigrams, and is thus akin to *Iambi* 7 and 9 which both portray talking statues.

The simplicity of the description of the statue of Apollo contrasts strongly with the elaborate technical detail of the description of Zeus in *Iamb* 6. The technical niceties of *Iamb* 6 are a virtuoso effort, but they are incongruous in the context. If, as Dawson suggests, there were ancient guide books which contained this kind of information, the *Iamb* would serve as a nice parody of them. Unfortunately we have no evidence that these travel books existed. In the absence of such evidence it is safer to assume that Callimachus is giving us a parody of the whole genre of technical didactic poetry which was popular at the time, poetry such as Aratus and later Nicander wrote in earnest. If there were more fragments of the text we could be more sure of the interpretation. As it is we can only rely on parallels with the other *Iambi* where the form and content of different genres are combined in unexpected ways.

Iamb 7 (fr. 197)

Iambi 7-11 present special critical problems because there is even less remaining of them than the other *Iambi*. Several

---

[58] R. Pfeiffer, "The Image of the Delian Apollo and Apolline Ethics," *Journal of the Warburg and Courtauld Institutes* 15 (1927) 22 ff.

of these poems appear to be bold departures from the traditional forms of the genre.

The seventh *Iamb* has the same epodic metrical form as the sixth, and a dialect which is largely Doric.[59] Like 1, 2, and 4 it includes a fable, the *aition* of the cult of Hermes Perpheraios at Ainos. Our text of the poem is poor beyond hope, but, as if to compensate, the summary of the story in the *Dieg.* is particularly detailed. It tells us that before Epeius made the Wooden Horse he produced a statue of Hermes which was swept away by a much-swollen Scamander, and carried into the sea off Ainos, in Thrace, where some fishermen drew it up in their net. They were very displeased with their catch, and attempted to break it up into firewood, but for all their efforts, they succeeded in doing no more than making the form of a wound on its shoulder. Next they attempted to burn it whole, but the fire merely played around it. Finally, conceding defeat, they threw it back into the sea. When they drew it up yet again, it finally occurred to them that the image was divine and they established a shrine for it on the shore where they offered it first fruits, passing it around one to another. Later, on the command of Apollo, they received it into their city and honored it equally to their own gods (*Dieg.* VIII 1-20).

Commentators have noted that the content of this story closely resembles the legend of Dionysus Phallen in Methymna (Pf., I, 193), and therefore it may be considered a traditional Greek story-type, "eine richtige Fischererzählung," as Puelma (228) aptly puts it. The aitiological story, which always held a particular fascination for Callimachus, is a not untypical Aesopic type.[60] The location of the action, at Ainos, is perhaps intended as a pun on the genre (194.6).

The poem begins,

'Ερμᾶς ὁ Περφεραῖος, Αἰνίων θεός,
    ἔμμι τῶ φυγαίχμα
. . .] πάρεργον ἱπποτέκτον[ος·

Hermes the Perpheraian, the god of Ainos
I am, a bywork of the battle-shunning
horse-maker.

(197.1-3)

Epeius is called battle-shunning (197.2) in reference to the tradition that he was a physical coward.[61] In recalling this charge, Callimachus may wish to emphasize the special role of the artist in society. Archilochus, a professional soldier, showed his contempt for traditional military values by freely admitting that he once left his shield behind in battle, as does Horace after him.[62] Epeius also joined in the patriotic cause, and like the others, his best weapon was his art, which ultimately succeeded where the conventional swordsmen failed.

The emphasis quickly shifts away from the artist to the statue he made, which, in epigram style, narrates the story itself. Unfortunately, the condition of the text does not allow us to see much about Callimachus' handling of the narrative.

At line 39, where *P. Oxy.* 611 begins to provide half lines, someone, presumably a fisherman (Pf., I, 194), is described as looking up at the sky and concluding a speech in which the subject of fire arises (197.40). He is doubtless exhorting his mates to burn the Herm, which appears to them to have no intrinsic value. Line 42 perhaps chronicles their attempt,

πυρδάνω 'πὺ λεπ[τῶ·

on slender kindling

(197.42).

The remains of lines 43-44,

κἠγὼ 'π' ἐκείναν [
ταῖς ἐμαῖς ἐπῳδα[ῖς·

and I against that
with my songs

(197.43-44)

seem to imply that the Herm halted his own destruction by magical incantations, a detail unfortunately omitted by the *Dieg.*

The remains of lines 45-51 relate to that part of the story in which the Herm is hurled once again into the sea and is pulled out a second time. At this point the text fails completely and we are indebted entirely to the *Dieg.* for our knowledge of the conclusion.

---

[61] Com. asdsp. 31 K.; Lycophron 930. There is also a counter-tradition that Epeius joined the men in the horse at last (Vergil *Aen.* 2.264 f.).
[62] Archil 6 D.³ = 5 W. Horace C. 2.7.

This poem would seem more at home in the *Aitia* than here among the *Iambi*. Like *Aitia* fr. 114 (above p. 35) it is in form an extended epigram. Metrical inscriptions in which objects such as a tombstone or statue-base speak in the first person can be found as early as the seventh century B.C. and are not rare in iambic meters. Dawson describes a sixth century statue-base which contains an inscription in five iambic trimeters which says that it supported a statue of Phoebus, names the dedicator, the occasion and the cause of the dedication.[63] Sepulchral inscriptions often give biographical information about the deceased. The Herm's elaborate discussion of his own origins grows out of this tradition. Like the *ekphrasis* of *Iamb* 6, it is something entirely new in the iambic genre.

Iamb 8 (fr. 198)

Iamb 8 is the third in the series of bold experiments. It is, according to the *Dieg.* (VIII 21-24), an *epinicion* in honor of Polycles of Aigina, written in iambic trimeters and Ionic dialect. Within the epinician form the poem contains an aitiological story: the origin of the Hydrophoria. The *Dieg.* tells us that the contest originated when the Argonauts, who had landed on Aigina, vied with one another in an effort to fetch water more speedily (*Dieg.* VIII 28-32).

All that remains of the text itself is the first line,

'Αργώ κοτ' ἐμπνέοντος ἤκαλον νότου

Once the Argo, when the south wind was blowing peacefully

(198.1).

It is impossible to say what Callimachus did with the story. If he meant to have some fun playing with the epinician genre the poems of Pindar would surely have been his target. Pindar wrote eleven of his extant poems in honor of Aeginetan victors, nearly all of which are concerned with the heroic past of Aigina as Callimachus is here.[64] The scholiast on Pindar's *I.* 2.9 attributes the following lines to Callimachus, which may come from *Iamb* 8,

---

[63] *BCH* 47 (1920) 227-236; Dawson 82-83.
[64] *O.* 8; *P.* 8; *I.* 5, 8; *N.* 3, 4, 5, 6, 7, 8; *Paean* 6.

οὐ γὰρ ἐργάτιν τρέφω
τὴν Μοῦσαν, ὡς ὁ Κεῖος Ὑλίχου νέπους

I do not nourish a worker Muse
like the Cean child of Hylichos.

(fr. 222)

The reference here is to the epigrammatist Simonides of Ceos, one of Pindar's arch-rivals. There is no obvious way to fit these lines into the account of the poem offered by the *Dieg.*

It is also worth noting that Apollonius of Rhodes includes a brief description of the original Hydrophoria in *Argonautica* 4.1765-1772. There is no way of knowing which version was written first or whether one was meant as a comment on the other.

Iamb 9 (fr. 199)

Iamb 9, like 8, is written in stichic iambic trimeters, but the dialect is Doric. As in *Iambs* 6 and 7, which are also Doric, a statue is the center of attention. In this case it is an ithyphallic Hermes.[65] The Herm's rampant sexuality reflects and comically amplifies Callimachus' state in the third *Iamb* and that of the grammatodidaskalos in the fifth. These associations tend to support B. Lavagnini's suggestion that fr. 221 also be assigned to this poem,[66]

αἰτοῦμεν εὐμάθειαν Ἑρμᾶνος δόσιν

We ask for easy-learning, the gift of Hermes

(221)

If this is accepted, Hermes may assume the role of teacher as well as lover.

According to the *Dieg.*, the Herm is asked by a lover of the handsome youth Philetadas if he is in such a condition on account of this same youth. The Herm replies that he is of Tyrsenian origin and that his state is explained by a mystic story (*Dieg.* VIII 33-39), which he presumably narrates to his interlocutor. The *Dieg.* also tells us that at the conclusion of the story the Herm accuses his interlocutor of loving Philetadas for evil purposes (VIII 39-40).

---

[65] Dawson 64.

[66] B. Lavagnini, "Osservazioni ai Giambi di Callimaco," *AAPal* 19 (1935) 8.

Like *Iamb* 7, 9 is an extended epigram. Here the statue is engaged in a dialogue with a passerby as in *Aitia* fr. 114 (see above p. 35). Into this form Callimachus works two strands he has been weaving into the *Iambi*: the aitiological story and the public remonstration about sexual behavior. The statue's sudden turning on the interlocutor provides a surprise twist at the end.

Iamb 10 (fr. 200)

In *Iamb* 10 the Ionic dialect reappears in iambic trimeter, as does aitiological tale. The *Dieg.* tells us that the poet explains why Aphrodite Castnia at her shrine at Aspendus in Pamphylia accepts the sacrifice of pigs. Mopsus, a leader of the Pamphylians, vowed that he would sacrifice to Aphrodite whatever he caught first. Since he caught a boar and fulfilled his vow, the Pamphylians continue the practice to this day. The poet also praises Artemis of Eretria because she refuses no sacrifices (VIII 41-IX 11).

Beyond its general aitiological character there is nothing in the summary to link this poem to the other *Iambi*, except perhaps its interest in Aphrodite who is also featured in *Iamb* 11.

Iamb 11 (fr. 201)

In *Iamb* 11 the dialect returns to Doric and the meter is a new variation of the iambic, a pentapody. The summary of the *Dieg.* follows: The proverb, "the possessions of Connarus may be snatched up" is quoted mistakenly. We must read "of Connidas," for the following reason. Connidas, a metic in Selinos, who had grown rich from the prostitution trade, used to say that he would divide his property between Aphrodite and his friends. But when he died, his will was found to say, "the possessions of Connidas may be snatched up," and the people coming out of the theater grabbed up his property (*Dieg.* IX 12-23). Here then we have another aitiological tale with clearly immoral overtones.

The first line,

'Αλλ' οὐ τὸν Ὑψᾶν, ὃς τὸ σᾶμά μευ

But not, by Hypsas, who (goes by) my tomb,

(201.1)

indicates that a sepulchral monument narrates some or all of the poem. The Hypsas is the principal river of Selinos. Line 1 echoes a formula very common in funerary epigrams, and therefore 11 belongs with *Iambi* 7 and 9 which are also extended epigrams in Doric dialect. Like 9 it has an element of obscenity and like 10 it has to do with Aphrodite.

The proverb about Connidas has been preserved in two other sources which exhibit at least 3 versions of the name.[67] It is impossible to guess which of these may have been known to the poet. The literal-minded *Dieg.* puts a spotlight on Callimachus' correction of Connidas' name, but its emphasis may be misplaced. The poem may be less an exercise in learning than a ribald account of the probating of Connidas' will, as the whole town pursues his prostitutes. Callimachus is not the sort to overlook the humerous possibilities of this situation. The pimp is a stock figure from new comedy who is likely to have received comic treatment.

Iamb 12 (fr. 202)

The twelfth *Iamb* both continues Callimachus' experiments with the iambic genre and returns to the themes of the first, Hipponactean *Iambi*. The dialect is Ionic and the meter, catalectic trochaic trimeter. The appearance of trochaic meter in the midst of iambi gave rise to several mistaken theories about the place of this poem within the collection. These were reviewed above (p. 4-6). In form the poem is a birthday song. The *Dieg.* (IX 25-28) tells us that the poem was written for Leon, an acquaintance of the poet, for the seventh day celebration of his daughter. The poem tells the story of a contest among the gods over who could give the best gift to Hera's daughter Hebe, on the occasion of the seventh day celebration of her birth. Apollo's gift of song prevails over all the others (*Dieg.* IX 28-31).

As in 1, 2, and 4 the story which the poem contains has a direct relationship to present circumstances. Leon's little girl must be equated with Hebe and Callimachus with Apollo. As in *Iamb* 4 Callimachus begins the poem by introducing the human part of the analogy first. In this case he provides an elaborate invocation in which he calls upon various deities who might take an interest in such an event as Artemis of Amnisos (202.1-8), the Moiroi (202.9), their mother Themis (202.12), and upon the inspirers of his songs, Apollo (202.15 ff.) and the Muse (202.20). τῇ μικκῇ

---

[67] Pf. I 199.

(202.20) is probably the little girl in whose honor the poem is ostensibly written.

When the invocation is complete, Callimachus begins to describe the divine part of the equation, the celebration for Hebe. The Olympians were all invited to the celebration (202.23), and the poet tells of the lovely gifts brought by each.

All we know of father Zeus' present is that it was 'not bad' (202.26), but the description of the exquisite workmanship of Athena's gifts is better preserved,

πολλὰ τεχνήεντα ποικ[ίλ]α γλ[υφῇ [68]
παίχν[ια] Τριτωνὶς ἤνεικεν κόρ[

Many multicolored toys worked with a knife
the Tritonian maiden brought.

(202.27-28)

Poseidon (202.29) [69] brought toys more valuable than gold (202.33), while Demeter, still mourning for her stolen child (202.38-39), and perhaps Hephaestus, if he is the ἐργάτης of line 43, brought or sent other gifts. And so the gods vied with one another over the presents,

. . . γ]λυκεῖαν ἀλλήλοις ἔριν
θ]έντες ἡμ[ι]λλῶντο δω[τί]νη[ς πέρι.

In sweet contention with one another
they competed in gift-giving.

(202.45-46)

Delian Apollo enters the competition last at line 47. In an unusual parody of divine invocation, Apollo apparently addresses himself, asking for the tools of the craft of poetry,[70]

χρεὼ σοφῆς ὦ Φοῖβε . . . τέχνης

There is need, Oh Phoebus, for your wise skill.

(202.56)

---

[68] γλυφῇ if Barber's emendation is correct, recalls Callimachus' interest in the tools of craftsmanship already expressed in 197.5 where he mentions the σκέπαρνον with which Epeius carved the Hermes.

[69] See Callimachus' description of Poseidon in fr. 384.

[70] It was once thought that Apollo's speech extended only from lines 54-55 and that the poet himself spoke lines 56 ff., but a version of the text based on the Mich. Papyrus (see below n. 71) makes it clear that Apollo continues speaking at least until line 70.

Unusual good fortune has provided us with an almost complete text of the remaining portion of his speech.[71] Line 57 completes the thought of 56, asserting that his craft, that of song, will triumph over the products of mere handwork,

ἥτις Ἡφαίστεια νικήσει καλά.

which will conquer the lovely things of Hephaestus.

(202.57)

This is followed by a discourse on the evils of wealth which resembles that of the third *Iamb* (193.6 ff.). Here, Apollo, as befits an oracular god, talks about a future state of affairs,

αὐτίκα χρυσὸν μὲν Ἰνδικοὶ κύνες
βυσσόθεν μύρμηκες οἴσουσι πτεροῖς·
πολλάκις καὶ φαῦλον οἰκήσει δόμον
χρυσός, ἀρχαίους δ' ἀτιμήσει[. . .
καὶ Δίκην καὶ Ζῆνα καὶ[. . .
ὑπτίῳ παίσαντες ἄνθρωποι ποδί
χρυσὸν αἰνήσουσι τίμιον[. . .

At once Indic dogs, the ants,
will bring gold from deep within on their wings.
Often gold will inhabit an evil home
and it will dishonor the ancient [   ].
Having struck Dike and Zeus with inverted foot,
men will praise honored gold.

(202.58-64)

The gold which Apollo castigates is also the substance of other gods' gifts (202.65 ff.), which though perfected with artisans' tools (202.66),[72] time in its forward march will destroy (202.67). Against the immorality and impermanence of physical wealth, Apollo dramatically sets his own gift,

ἡ δ' ἐμὴ τῇ παιδὶ καλλίστη δόσις
ἔστ' ἐμὸν γένειον ἀγνεύῃ τριχός
καὶ ἐρίφοις χαίρωσιν ἄρπαγ[ες λ]ύκ[ο]ι

---

[71] P. Mich inv. 4947 edited by C. Bonner in *Aegyptus* 31 (1951) 133-137, reprinted with emendations and notes in Pf. II Addenda and Corrigenda 118-119.

[72] There was an earlier reference to the tools of craft at line 27. ἡ σμίλη is a tool for cutting or carving. In *AP* 7.429, a sculptor's chisel.

But my gift to the child is most beautiful
As long as my cheek is free of hair
and plundering wolves enjoy kids. . . .[73]

(202.68-70)

Our text for the remainder of the poem is in pitiful condition. The *Dieg.* (IX 28) asserts that Apollo won the competition
and this seems to be confirmed in line 75.

By line 78 the poet has begun to speak in his own voice again,
perhaps to say that he will fashion a song for Leon's daughter
(202.78) in imitation of the god's for Hebe (202.77). Line 82
seems to be a re-invocation of Artemis. Although we do not know
how long the poem was in its original form, the repetition of the
opening theme suggests that it did not proceed much beyond the
86 partially preserved verses (Dawson 135).

By returning in his conclusion to the occasion on which he is
presenting his own poem, Callimachus seems to give special emphasis
to the equation of his own song with that of Apollo. Apollo's
presentation was made in the course of a competition among peers.
One may assume that Callimachus sees himself as pre-eminent
among his own peers. It is not accidental that these sentiments
are expressed after a series of *Iambi* featuring statues (6, 7, 9, and
11), which will decay long before his song.

In 12 then we come back to the world of the Hipponactean
Iambi (1, 2, 3, 4) where illustrative tales reflect on current events,
where the poet has rivals and where the value of song over wealth
needs to be defended.

Iamb 13 (fr. 203)

Iamb 13 is a natural development from the movement in 12
back toward the Hipponactean posture of *Iamb* 1. Like the first
Iamb, the thirteenth is written in a literary Ionic dialect in stichic
choliambic trimeters. Also like 1, 13 is addressed to an audience
of unfriendly contemporaries (*Dieg.* IX 33-34). In this poem,
however, Callimachus appears to speak for himself.

The poem begins with an invocation and a libation for the lovely
Muses and for Apollo, who is prominent in the first and twelfth
Iambi. Following the invocation, the poem can be divided into

---

[73] G. Luck, "Kids and Wolves: Callimachus fr. 202.69-70," *CQ* N.S. 9
(1959) 34-37, gives these lines an obscene interpretation.

three sections: the attack of Callimachus' adversaries against the poet (203.11-22); Callimachus' defense (203.24-49); and the poet's comments on the unfortunate effects such divisiveness has on the literary community as a whole (203.50-66).

The adversaries' attack begins in our text at line 11,

> [οὔτ'] Ἴωσι συμμείξας
> οὔτ' Ἔφεσον ἐλθών, ἥτις ἐστι[. . .
> Ἔφεσον, ὅθεν περ οἱ τὰ μέτρα μέλλοντες
> τὰ χωλὰ τίκτειν μὴ ἀμαθῶς ἐναύονται·

> Neither having mingled with Ionians
> nor gone to Ephesus, which is . . .
> Ephesus, where those who are about
> to give birth to choliambs are set afire,
> if they are clever.

> (203.11-14)

Here they charge that Callimachus has not shown proper regard for his model, Hipponactean choliambs. These remarks presumably refer to the style of the 12 preceding poems some of which are rather daring developments of the iambic genre.

After this general complaint, the adversaries describe a specific violation Callimachus has made against the tradition,

> τοῦτ' ἐμπ[έ]πλεκται καὶ λαλευσ[. . .
> Ἰαστὶ καὶ Δωριστὶ καὶ τὸ σύμμεικ[τον.

> This is interwoven and babbling . . .
> Ionian and Dorian and the mixed dialect.

> (203.17-18)

Callimachus is said to weave together Greek dialects [74] with results that could be described with a form of λαλέω, a word which Callimachus has often used himself to characterize bad poets such as Euhemerus in *Iamb* 1 (191.11) and the writers whom he criticizes in *Iamb* 2 (192.14). Hipponax, in contrast, uses only the Ionic dialect.

---

[74] The metaphor of poets weaving words is as old as Homer and was a particular favorite of Pindar (*N.*4.94; *O.*6.87). The poets use the image in a positive sense. It is not until Plato that the metaphor becomes pejorative. He describes how poets mix up animal cries, the voices of men and musical instruments with ridiculous and illogical results (Pl. *Lg.* 669D). Such a cacophony could easily be described with a form of λαλέω (203.17).

At line 19, the attack against Callimachus becomes more personal. If his friends have any sense themselves they will bind him and pour out a libation for the sake of his mental health (203.19-21). This picture recalls Callimachus' earlier portrait of a mad man in the first *Iamb* (191.78), and the poet who was μάργος in *Iamb* 3 (193.38-39).

The speech of the adversaries appears to end at line 22 and Callimachus' reply begins two lines later (203.24). In this speech Callimachus clearly intends to recall that of Hipponax in *Iamb* 1.

ὦ λῷστ', ἐρῆμος[   ] ἡ ῥῆσις
ἀκου ... [   ] ... πέπλ[ον

My good man, abandoned ... the speech
listen ...

(203.24-25)

Following Hipponax, Callimachus addresses his critics as λῷστε (203.24 and 191.33), calls the speech itself a ῥῆσις (203.24 and 191.31) and bids his audience to listen with the verb ἀκούω (203.25 and 191.1). Connections with the first *Iamb* can be found even where the text is most lacunose. Lobel noticed that lines 25-26 seem to end with precisely the same words as 191.91-92 although neither has any context which could reveal its meaning.[75] Furthermore, ἀπεμπολῇ κόψας (203.27) recalls κονδύλῳ καπηλεῦσ[αι (191.89). Here also both phrases are out of context and the meaning of juxtaposing commerce and physical violence is by no means obvious.

At line 30 Callimachus finally begins the argument promised by the *Dieg.* (IX 34-36). He defends himself vigorously against the charges of *polyeideia* i.e. of writing in many different genres, by citing the example of Ion of Chios, a fifth century author of an impressive variety of literature.[76] Callimachus categorically denies that the gods have allotted each poet a single genre (203.30-33) and lists some of the many genres in which Ion wrote (203.44-47).

---

[75] Pf. I 171.
[76] Schol. (RV) Ar. *Pax* 835.

The third part of the poem begins in our text at lines 203.52-53
where the poet describes what fierce rivalry has done to the present
literary community,

ἀ]οιδὸς ἐς κέρας τεθύμωται
κοτέω]ν ἀοιδῷ . . .

The poet is furious to the point of using the horn,
angry at a poet . . .[77]

(203.52-53).

and one poet brands another a slave (203.54-56). Personal animosity
between poets is also reflected in the first *Iamb* where Hipponax
asks the bickering literati to co-operate and in the second where
Aesop compares the voices of various poets to animal voices.

These expressions of ill will cause the Muses to desert the whole
community, fearing for their reputations,

φαύλοις ὁμι[λ]εῖ[ν . . .] παρέπτησαν
καὐταὶ τρομεῦσαι μὴ κακῶς ἀκούσωσι·

To associate with common types . . . They
flew past fearing that they
might gain a bad repute.

(203.58-59)

This recalls the starved Muses of *Iamb* 1 (191.92-93). Here it
is the poets themselves who manage to scrape up only the most
meager living (203.60-62), but Callimachus' point is essentially
the same, divisiveness is destroying the poetic community, and
poets are in bad repute. It is perhaps no joke then when Hipponax
returns to the world above in *Iamb* 1 to tell the story of Bathycles'
Cup, a plea for peace.

It is impossible to say whether Callimachus himself is answering
criticism which had actually been leveled against some of the
Iambi already in circulation, or whether he is posturing here—
setting up his defense before the critics could get started. It is
clear, however, that *Iamb* 13 comes full-circle round to *Iamb* 1
in meter, dialect, dramatic setting and attitude. It would seem
in light of this that 13 was the original end point of the collection
of *Iambi*.

---

[77] Horace uses this figure of the angry bull specifically in reference to
the anger of an iambicist (*Ep*. 6.11.14).

The *Iambi* and *Polyeideia*

The salient feature of the *Iambi* as a group is the variety of its poems which differ from one another in form, meter, dialect, and length. Callimachus justifies this feature of his style in the concluding *Iamb* where he presents critics who charge him with *polyeideia*, of writing many different kinds of poetry. While this charge may be aimed at the poet's entire corpus, it is likely that it refers directly and exclusively to the *Iambi* themselves.

It is easy to see what Callimachus' critics had in mind when they made this charge. The *Iambi* include many types of poems generally considered distinct. *Iambi* 1 and 3 are harangues against *aischrokerdia*; 2 and 4 are moralizing fables; 5 appears to be Hipponactean invective; 6 combines the *propemptikon* and *ekphrasis*. 7-11 are all *aitia* but of different kinds. 7 and 9 are narrated by talking statues on the model of sepulchral epigrams such as 11 certainly is. 8 is an *epinicion*; 10, a cult *aition*. The twelfth is a variety of birthday song and finally the thirteenth is the poet's personal justification of his work. These various types of poems are written in five different metrical schemes and three different dialects.

It is the impression of modern critics, notably Dawson and Puelma, that these variations are far from random, rather, they have been carefully orchestrated according to conscious aesthetic principles. The alternations of form, meter, dialect, and length are calculated to achieve an effect of a *taxis ataktos*, an ever interesting and seemingly casual variety or *poikilia* controlled by the artist to create an aesthetically pleasing whole.[78]

Obviously the fragmentary state of the text severely limits what can be said in defense of this hypothesis, but some principles of organization emerge despite the handicap. The first five poems are Hipponactean in aspect, Ionic in dialect, choliambic in meter and critical in character. The first 4 are stichic and the epodic fifth signals a change in character which appears in *Iamb* 6, and pervades 7 and 8. These three poems are experimental in form and not obviously critical. 6 and 7, which concern themselves with statues are Doric in dialect and Epodic in meter. 8, the *epinicion*, is Ionic and stichic. The change in meter in 8 signals a change in character which appears in *Iamb* 9 and pervades the final five

---

[78] Dawson, 141-144; Puelma, 335.

poems, which, like 1-5 are concerned with morality, eros, and literature. In this group the "statue" poems 9 and 11 are Doric, while the others are Ionic. Unlike the opening poems which are consistently choliambic, meter in the final group changes frequently, becoming increasingly unusual: iambic trimeter gives way to iambic pentapody, which yields in turn to acatalectic trochaic tetrameter, and returns abruptly to choliambic trimeter in *Iamb* 13.[79]

Dawson (142) has also shown that the *Iambi* were organized by theme in an architectonic manner familiar from Roman poetry books such as Horace's *Epodes* and Virgil's *Eclogues*. The first *Iamb* is clearly meant to introduce the whole series and the 13th, to end it. The 2nd and the 4th are both Aesopic fables, the 3d and the 5th, both personal attacks in erotic contexts. The 7th and 9th feature talking Herms, the 8th and 10th, heroic myth. *Iambi* 6 and 12 are both personal poems "standing at the close of a varied half dozen." Only the 11th *Iamb*, the epitaph of Connarus, is not included in this structure. It should be linked with the talking Herms in 7 and 9 to produce this pleasingly asymetrical scheme:

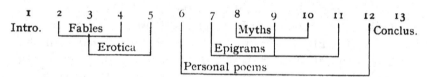

Callimachus himself must have seen the *Iambi* as an organized whole, for in *Iamb* 13 when he justifies the diversity of his work by the example of Ion of Chios who wrote in many different genres, he describes the summation of Ion's achievement this way:

... ἐντελές τε τὸ χρῆμα
... ἀνεπλάσθη

The thing
was made perfect.

(203.48-49).

The verb πλάσσω (203.49) appears in the first *Iamb* as a metaphor for making poetry (191.10), and suggests an identification of the

---

[79] Dawson, 143, has constructed a chart listing the number, length, dialect and general character of each *Iambus*.
blz. 50.

poet as craftsman. As the *Dieg.* indicates (IX 37-38), this metaphor had been much more fully developed here.

The idea that making poetry is a craft rather than an unmeditated act of inspiration is at least as old as the fifth century. In the *Frogs* e.g. Aristophanes uses carpentering metaphors to describe Euripides' poetic technique and Euripides plans to use a whole carpenter's shop for testing Aeschylus' tragedies.[80] Whether these metaphors already have the status of technical terms in a new vocabulary of literary criticism or whether they are the original fruits of Aristophanes' invention,[81] they seem to be informed by the sophistic view that rhetoric, and by extension all writing, could be analyzed in a systematic way.

The Sophistic view was condemned by Plato. In the *Ion* e.g. Socrates compels Ion the Rhapsode [82] to admit that the rhapsodic art is not a true *techne*, such as prophecy or arithmatic, because Ion is not able to interpret all poets, but only Homer. Socrates claims that interpreting poetry requires inspiration rather than *techne* because art itself requires inspiration:

> According to divine fate, each (poet) is able to succeed in writing only that towards which the Muse has propelled him; one writes dithyrambs, one, *encomia*; one *hypochemata*, another epic, and yet another, iambs. And each is poor at writing in the other genres. For they do not compose these works by poetic skill (τέχνη) but by divine power, for if they knew how to write in one genre by virtue of skill, they would know how to write in all the others. (Pl. *Ion* 534 C).

In stating that genres are not allotted to poets by the gods (203.30-32) and that he is free to write, like the poet Ion, in whatever genre he wishes (*Dieg.* IX 35-38), Callimachus is specifically answering Socrates' contention that poets compose only through inspiration.

The craftsman poet does not have the same attitude toward his creation as the inspired poet. The crafts metaphor implies

---

[80] *Ra.* 799-802; 814-829; 881; 902.
J. D. Denniston, "Technical Terms in Aristophanes," *C.Q.* 21 (1927) 113-121 esp. 114.

[81] Denniston, above n. 80, and D. L. Clayman, "The Origins of Greek Literary Criticism and the *Aitia* Prologue," *W.S.* 90 (1977) 27-34.

[82] Not Ion of Chios, but a rhapsode who has the same name and comes from Ephesus (350A) Hipponax's native city and the source of the iambic tradition Callimachus is accused of ignoring.

a distance between poet and poem which allows critical attitudes to develop. Without such distance, parody, the principal critical technique of Callimachus' *Iambi* would be impossible.

Callimachus' critics may well complain that his *Iambi* are not purely Ephesian. He never intended them to be. In *Iamb* 1 Hipponax is dead. He appears as a ghost of the past to invoke a literary norm which is instantly violated. Hipponax, who was one of the most obscene of early Greek poets is there to play the role of a holier-than-thou Cynic diatribist, and neither Hipponax nor the Cynics escapes from the situation unscathed. Hipponax is also imitated in *Iamb* 5 where Callimachus substitutes Lykophronesque riddles for unseemly invective. In *Iamb* 3 Hipponax is put aside and the ostentatious moralizing of contemporary choliambographers is debunked when made to express the anguish of a failed love affair. Non-iambic literary forms are reduced to absurdity in 4 (rhetoric), 6 (*ekphrasis, propemptikon*, and perhaps technical didactic verse), 7 and 9 (epigram).

The writing of parodies such as these depends on the poet's ability to separate form from content. By mixing up the form of one genre with the content of another, Callimachus demonstrates the emptiness of both.[83]

Aristophanes' parody of Aeschylus and Euripides in the *Frogs* signals the death of tragedy at the end of the fifth century. Similarly, Callimachus' *Iambi* could exist only after the old Ionic forms and the other genres he exploits had lost their vitality. By the third century, the poetic genres of the archaic and classical ages had long since peaked. What Alexandrian could write an Homeric epic or an Aeschylean tragedy or an Hipponactean iamb and expect to be taken seriously? Any Hellenistic poet worthy of the name had to invent new forms or radically alter the old ones to make themselves some working space. The doctrine of genre purity, which is the position of Callimachus' critics in *Iamb* 13, led only to sterile imitation.

Callimachus' *Iambi* are both a statement of the Alexandrians' literary dilemma and a solution to it in the form of a redefinition of the iambic genre. Their chaos of form and content reflect literary reality as Callimachus perceived it. Their wit, variety, detachment, literateness, and artistic organization create a new life for the genre which was realized ultimately in Rome.

---

[83] For a general discussion of this effect, G. D. Kiremidjian, "The Aesthetics of Parody," *Journal of Aesthetics and Art Criticism* 28 (1970) 231-42.

The Mele fr. 226-229

Following the thirteenth *Iamb* in the *Dieg.* and the principal papyrus, *P. Oxy.* 1011, are four poems which may or may not be *Iambi*. The controversy surrounding them has been outlined above (pp. 4-7).

Unlike the first 13, three of these four have individual titles. The untitled poem is the first, fr. 226. Taking his clue from the summary of the *Dieg.*, Pfeiffer calls it ΠΡΟΣ ΤΟΥΣ ΩΡΑΙΟΥΣ, "To the Beautiful Boys." Its meter is phalaecean hendecasyllabic, and it seems to have described the Lemnian massacre. The *Dieg.* says that Lemnos, once happy, had bad luck when the women attacked the men. Therefore even you, beautiful boys, look to the future (*Dieg.* X 1-5). It has in common with some *Iambi* its general format—a story of a past event told to reflect on the present.

The second poem, fr. 227, is entitled *Pannychis*, "The All-night Festival." It is written in an asinartetic meter which combines an iambic dimeter with an ithyphallic and is known as a 14-syllable Euripidean. The *Dieg.* (X 6-9) describes it as a drinking song for the Dioscuri which also celebrates Helen and asks her to accept the sacrifice. The poet urges his drinking companions to stay awake. The opening lines,

Ἔνεστ' Ἀπόλλων τῷ χορῷ· τῆς λύρης ἀκούω·
καὶ τῶν Ἐρώτων ᾐσθόμην· ἔστι κἀφροδίτη.

Apollo is in the chorus. I hear the lyre.
I sensed the Erotes, and Aphrodite is here,

(227.1-2)

recall Hymn 2 where Callimachus describes the arrival of Apollo. Other fragmentary lines tell of the rewards due to the man who is able to keep awake (227.5-7).

The third poem (fr. 228) is the "Deification of Arsinoe," wife of Ptolemy II Philadelphus who died in 270 B.C. The poet says that Arsinoe was snatched up by the Dioscuri and that an altar and *temenos* were established for her near the *emporion* (*Dieg.* X 10-13).

As the poem begins Callimachus calls on Apollo to take the lead (228.1-4). An apostrophe to Arsinoe follows (228.5-8). The longest fragment (228.42-75) tells how Arsinoe's sister Philotera, already dead herself, learned the news from the smoke of the funeral pyre.

The last poem (fr. 229) is the "Branchus," written in choriambic pentameters. The *Dieg.* gives a brief summary: Apollo comes from Delos into a place near Miletus which is called the Sacred Wood, where Branchos is (*Dieg.* X 14-17).

From the fragments, we can see that the poem begins with an address to Phoebus and Zeus, founders of Didyma (229.1). A prophecy of Apollo follows (229.2-8), and then Branchus' receiving the gift of prophecy (229.9). In 229.10-11, Branchus founds the shrine and then the poet greets Apollo Delphinius (229.12). How the poem develops after this point, we do not know.

The arguments for excluding these poems from the collection of the *Iambi* are basically these: (1) They are written in non-iambic meters. (2) Three of the four have individual titles while none of the thirteen *Iambi* (fr. 191-203) have titles. (3) Their subject matter is not iambic in character. (4) None of them is cited by ancient authorities as coming from the *Iambi.*[84] (5) They have no themes in common with the first thirteen poems, which share many themes among them, and they lie outside *Iamb* 13 which is clearly a formal conclusion to the group of poems beginning with fr. 191.

Ardizzoni[85] has objected to point 1, the metrical argument. He notes that Horace uses asinartetic meters which are partly iambic in *Epodes* 11 and 13 and that Catullus and Martial use Phalaecean hendecasyllables in obviously iambic contexts. He has no parallels, however, for iambic use of anapests or choriambs. Point 2 on the titles is the most objective and irrefutable of the arguments. Point 3, on the subject matter, is more subjective, but it is not so easily dismissed. It will not do to point out that subject matter of *Iambi* 6-8 and 10 is not obviously iambic either. 6-8 and 10 could be iambic in spirit, depending on the way the poet treats the subject at hand. In contrast fr. 227 on the deification of Arsinoe could not be iambic in spirit without insulting her husband Ptolemy II. It seems unlikely that Callimachus would

---

[84] See p. 6 above on the possibility that the Branchus poem was so cited.

[85] A. Ardizzoni, "Considerazioni sulla struttura del libro dei Giambi di Callimaco," *Misc. di studi alessandrini in memoria di Augusto Rostagni* (Torino 1963) 258-260.

want to do that. Point 4 on the lack of ancient citations is an argument *ex silentio* and therefore much the weakest of the five. Point 5 is a literary argument and is persuasive only if the reader accepts in its broad outline the interpretations of the *Iambi* and especially of *Iamb* 13 made above. There are a number of Roman parallels for concluding a series of poems with a defense of artistic principles.[86]

The best argument in favor of 17 *Iambi* is the fact that Horace wrote exactly seventeen *Epodes*. There are other reasons for thinking that Horace's *Epodes* are influenced in certain ways by the *Iambi*.[87] The use of asinartetic and hendecasyllabic meters by Horace and Catullus is the second best reason for thinking that the Romans knew 17 *Iambi*. These arguments, however, do not prove that it was Callimachus' intention to write a *Gedichtbuch* of seventeen *Iambi*. They only suggest that by the time a manuscript of Callimachus' *Iambi* reached Rome, some 300 years after the poems were written, the thirteen original *Iambi* were combined with four other of his shorter poems, in an omnibus edition of his work from which the *Dieg.* and *P. Oxy.* 1011 are descended. It has been said often that Callimachus himself made such an edition.[88] He or a later editor, would have found it convenient to place four shorter independent poems in a position after a collection of short poems, rather than scatter them among the larger ones. If the four were unrelated, we would not expect a single title such as 'Mele' to precede them in the manuscript and none does. Someone reading such a manuscript, however, might easily infer that there were 17 *Iambi*.

---

[86] v. e.g. Hor. *Sat.* 1.10; Propertius 2.34; Catullus 49-51, 116.
[87] See pp. 75 ff. below.
[88] Dawson 145-149; Pf. II xxxiii-xxxviii.

CHAPTER TWO

CALLIMACHUS AND EARLY IAMBI

At the heart of the Alexandrian literary debate was the question
of how a "modern" author should relate to his artistic predecessors.
In writing epic, for example, should one follow the model of Homer
or Hesiod? In writing iambic poems, Hipponax or Archilochus?
These questions were argued in theory by Callimachus and his
contemporaries, and the answers illustrated precisely whenever
an Alexandrian poet published his verse. Callimachus' techniques
in dealing with classical literature are nowhere illustrated more
clearly than in the *Iambi* where Callimachus can be observed
shaping a new conception of the iambic genre from a variety of
earlier literary traditions. This chapter is concerned with the
relations between Callimachus' *Iambi* and the work of Hipponax,
Archilochus, and Aristophanes.

Hipponax

Callimachus' first source for his conception of the iambic genre
is the sixth century Ephesian poet Hipponax. Callimachus makes
this point immediately by presenting the whole of the first *Iamb*
as a public harangue by a reincarnated Hipponax:

'Ακούσαθ' Ἱππώνακτος· οὐ γὰρ ἀλλ' ἥκω
ἐκ τῶν ὅκου βοῦν κολλύβου πιπρήσκουσιν,
φέρων ἴαμβον οὐ μάχην ἀείδοντα
τὴν Βουπάλειον . . .

Listen to Hipponax. For I have
come from those places where
an ox costs a penny, bringing
an iamb which does not sing of
the Boupalian battle. (191.1-4)

Callimachus has taken pains to give these lines a true Hipponactean
feel. The stichic choliambic meter is a favorite of Hipponax who
is usually credited with its invention.[1] In addition, the narrator's

---

[1] Suda s.v. Ἱππῶναξ and discussion, O. Masson, *Les Fragments du poète
Hipponax* (Paris 1962) 22. Hephaestion mentions Ananius as another possible
candidate (p. 17 Cons.).

The choliamb is an iambic trimeter in which the final iamb is replaced reference to himself by name in line one is a stylistic device found in Hipponax (24b D.^{3} = 32 W; Ar. 79b D.^{3} = 117 W; 32 D.^{3} = 37 W).[2] Even the joke about the low price of beef in Hades alludes to Hipponax who so often complains of his vexing poverty (25 D.^{3} = 34 W.; 29 D.^{3} = 36 W.).

Hipponax is not singing his old songs, however, about his fights with Bupalus (15 D.^{3} = 12 W.; 20 D.^{3} = 15 W.) but an iamb on a new subject, presumably the one we are about to hear, addressed to a group of Callimachus' colleagues in a contemporary Alexandrian setting.[3] The identity of the audience and the setting lead to the inescapable conclusion that this reincarnated Hipponax is none other than Callimachus himself.

The notion of Callimachus as a reborn Hipponax is given further scope by the references in *Iamb* 1 and 13 to Pythagoras and the Pythagorean doctrine of transmigration of souls. In the first *Iamb* these references take the form of somewhat lame witticisms. When Bathycles' son brings the Prize of Wisdom to Thales, he comes upon the sage scratching a geometrical figure in the ground (191.57-58), which, Callimachus tells us, Thales himself did not invent, but Euphorbus, the Phrygian (191.59), the very same Euphorbus whom Pythagoras once claimed was an earlier incarnation of himself (D.S. 10.6.1-3). The Pythagoreans had a well-known tendency to claim every possible mathematical discovery for their founder.[4] Since Pythagoras lived somewhat later in time than

---

by a spondee or troche, creating a somewhat asymmetrical effect. Like all early Ionian iambic verse, the composition of choliambs was governed by extraordinary precise laws (A. D. Knox, "The Early Iambus," *Philol.* 87 (1932) 18-39). As far as can be seen from the fragments, Callimachus follows the traditional rules with great accuracy. He observes all of the traditional caesuras, Porson's Law, and the Wilamowitz-Knoxian Bridge. In his strict attention to metrical rules and niceties Callimachus out-performs not only contemporary iambicists like Phoenix of Colophon and Herodas, but even Hipponax himself. Unlike his predecessor, Callimachus never allows pure iambs to appear among his choliambs (Masson 25, for instances in Hipponax), nor does he permit the final metrum of a choliambic line to consist entirely of spondees, rather he excludes the third anceps altogether (Masson 23-24). He rarely resolves longa.

[2] D.^{3} = the third edition of E. Diehl, *Anthologia Lyrica Graeca*^{3} (Leipzig 1949-52). W. = M. L. West, *Iambi et Elegi Graeci* I (Oxford 1971). West's numbering of Hipponax's poems is the same as Masson's (note 1 above). For discussion see A. Ardizzoni, "Callimaco Ipponatteo," *Annali della facoltà di lettere filosophia e magistero dell' Università di Cagliari* 28 (1960) 7.

[3] See page 11 above.

[4] D. L. 1.24-25 has an account of the controversies over the primacy of Thales or Pythagoras.

Thales,[5] Callimachus insists good-naturedly that the geometrical discoveries must have been made by that old soldier Euphorbus.

Another joke occurs at 191.61-63 where Callimachus makes fun of Pythagorean dietary habits, claiming that the Italians became vegetarians only because they could not afford meat.[6]

The jokes of *Iamb* 1 lead the way to a more serious concern for Pythagorean rebirth in *Iamb* 13. Here Callimachus defends his own literary practice of *polyeideia*, i.e. of writing in many different genres, by citing the example of Ion of Chios (*Dieg.* IX 33-36), who was known not only as a prolific writer in many genres, but also as a Pythagorean.[7] Since a Pythagorean soul has many incarnations, Ion, and by extension, Callimachus may be possessed by the identity of any literary predecessor and so they can write in any genre.

If Callimachus wishes to write iambs, he must only become a reborn Hipponax and look to Ephesus for inspiration,

"Εφεσον, ὅθεν περ οἱ τὰ μέτρα μέλλοντες
τὰ χωλὰ τίκτειν μὴ ἀμαθῶς ἐναύονται·

Ephesus, whence those who are
about to bring forth choliambs
are set afire, if they are clever.

(203.13-14 and 65-66)

A close look at the *Iambi* reveals how Callimachus interprets this idea.

Hipponax was well-known in antiquity for his waspish character. An epigram of Leonidas (*A.P.* 7.408) warns its readers to pass quietly by Hipponax's tomb lest they wake the sleeping wasp

---

[5] For information on the dates of Thales and Pythagoras see G. S. Kirk and J. E. Raven, *The Presocratic Philosophers* (Cambridge 1962) 74 and 217.

[6] See p. 14 above.

[7] Schol. (R.V.) Ar. *Pax* 835 quoted by Pf. I. 205. G. Huxley, "Ion of Chios," *GRBS* 6 (1965) 39.

Similarly in the prologue of the *Annales* Ennius describes a dream in which Homer's ghost appears to him expounding the Pythagorean doctrine of metempsychosis, and explaining how his soul, which had once passed into a peacock's body, has now entered Ennius'. Antipater (*A.P.* 7.75) claims that Homer entered the body of Stesichorus. C. O. Brink ("Hellenistic Worship of Homer," *AJP* 93 (1972) 558) suggests that Antipater and Ennius must have found the figure in a common Hellenistic source, although he does not know what it could be. Callimachus' first *Iamb*, where the poet appears as a reborn Hipponax and makes jokes about Pythagoreans, seems a likely candidate.

whose burning verses have the power to harm even in Hades. When Callimachus speaks of being "set afire" from Ephesus (203.14 and 66) he does not only mean that he is inspired by Hipponax to write choliambs, but also that he is enkindled with Hipponax's rage.

According to the epigram, Hipponax's rage was such that he even attacked his own parents. While the fragments that survive leave no trace of this particular incident they do contain plenty of abuse directed against personal acquaintances, most particularly against one Bupalus, a sculptor who, according to Pliny (*HN* 36. 4.11-13) produced a rather unattractive caricature of the poet. Tradition has it that Hipponax was enraged by Bupalus' work and caused the sculptor to commit suicide by the power of his invective. Pliny misdoubts some of the details of the story and so should we since it resembles so closely the tales about Archilochus and Lykambes. The feud with Bupalus, however, was certainly a literary reality in the poetry of Hipponax, and it is reflected in several framents which mention the name including one in which Hipponax announces his intention of bashing Bupalus in the eye (70 D.[3] = 120-121 W.) and another in which he accuses Bupalus of committing incest with his mother and of having relations with a woman named Arete (15 D.[3] = 12 W.).[8]

Callimachus' approach to invective is not obviously so blunt as Hipponax's. It is nevertheless true that Callimachus' *Iambi* are full of personal abuse directed at named or more probably pseudonamed individuals and that this abuse sometimes has an obscene character.

The cutting edge of Callimachus' invective is not often acknowledged. On the contrary, Callimachus is usually presented as a most mild-mannered iambicist. This view was first promulgated by F. Jung who in 1929 had not seen the *Dieg.*,

> Das die "Bupalosschlacht" des Hipponax sprichwörtlich geworden war, haben wir schon gesehen, ebenso, dass dieser den Choliambos zum typischen Spottverse geschaffen hatte. Im Gegensatz dazu betont also der Alexandriner, dass er dieses Mass zu anderen Zwecken gebrauchen will. Dem vornehmen Hofdichter passt der ruppige und proletarische Inhalt der Dichtungen des Joniers nicht.[9]

---

[8] Boupalus could perhaps be "bull-wrestler" a good name for a disreputable sort with whom Hipponax is always fighting.

[9] F. Jung, *Hipponax Redivivus* (Diss. Bonn 1929) 24.

Most commentators since Jung have re-echoed this view, although the evidence against it continues to mount.[10]

The difference between Callimachus' invective and Hipponax's can be best illustrated by comparing the fragments of Callimachus' fifth *Iamb* and Hipp. X D.[3] = 118 W. as we did in Chapt. I.[11] In this case, Hipponax's insults are altogether uncomplicated. He expresses his venom directly by means of degrading descriptions of his opponent's physical condition. In contrast, Callimachus prefers rather elaborate riddles. These riddles are certainly less blunt than Hipponax's outburst, but as we said above, they contain decidedly obscene innuendos.

There are clear indications that several of the other *Iambi* had more blatantly obscene subject matter. The ninth *Iamb* is narrated by an ithyphallic statue of Hermes who discusses the cause of his condition and accuses his interlocutor of harboring evil intentions toward a young man of his acquaintance. In *Iamb* 11, an articulate sepulchre tells the story of Connarus a wealthy pimp from Selinus who claimed that he would divide his property between Aphrodite and his friends but when his will was opened it was discovered that anyone could snatch up his goods.

The text of *Iambi* 9 and 11 is all but completely lost, and so it is not possible to say just how bluntly Callimachus allowed himself to speak on these less than polite subjects. There is an indication in *Iamb* 1, however, that he may have been very blunt indeed. Here at 191.98 it is possible to read the words τω κυσω, unfortunately out of context. A. Ardizzoni believes that this expression is part of a small section of obscene language which is intended to reinforce the image of Hipponax just at the moment of his departure for Hades.[12] Even if Ardizzoni is not correct here in emphasizing the Hipponactean context of this remark, the very presence of obscene language in *Iamb* 1, certainly raises the possibility that Callimachus could be obscene elsewhere in the *Iambi*, in his own or in another persona. This is especially so because *Iamb* 1 is in many ways an introduction to the themes and the tone of the whole group of *Iambi* which follow it.

Our scanty fragments of Hipponax do not reveal many of the

---

[10] As recently as P. M. Fraser, *Ptolemaic Alexandria* I (Oxford 1972) 733-734.

[11] See pages 30-31 above.

[12] Ardizzoni, n. 2 above, 9.

causes of that poet's outrage, but another Hellenistic epigram
suggests that Hipponax's outbursts were motivated by moral
judgements,

'Ο μουσοποιὸς ἐνθάδ' 'Ιππῶναξ κεῖται.
εἰ μὲν πονηρός, μὴ προσέρχευ τῷ τύμβῳ·
εἰ δ' ἐσσὶ κρήγυός τε καὶ παρὰ χρηστῶν,
θαρσέων καθίζευ, κἢν θέλῃς ἀπόβριξον.

The poet Hipponax lies here.
If you are base, do not approach
the tomb. If you are honorable
and of good stock, take heart; sit
down, and sleep if you wish. (Theoc.
19 Gow = A.P. 13.3)

A person who is κρήγυος is safe with Hipponax presumably
because Hipponax only attacked the πονηροί. It is likely that Hipponax claimed for himself the designation κρήγυος and compared
himself with the πονηροί around him, for this is precisely what
Callimachus does in *Iamb* 3. Callimachus describes his disillusionment with Euthydemos this way:

. . . κρηγύως ἐπαιδεύθην
. . . ἐ]φρόνησα τὠγαθὸν βλέψαι

I was educated nobly.
I thought I saw the good.

(193.30-31)

That the word κρήγυος has decidedly obscene innuendos (Plat.
Alcib. I 111E) suits the purposes of Hipponax and Callimachus
very well.

The notion of his own virtue pervades Callimachus' *Iambi*
and provides justification for both his outraged criticism of others
and for his histrionic displays of self-pity. The most elaborate
example of the latter can also be found in *Iamb* 3 in lines 32 following
where the poet concludes his plea to Euthydemos with a rhetorical
wish that he had been a eunuch devotee of Cybele instead of a
poet. Callimachus certainly learned this pose from Hipponax,
who complains eloquently about his poverty and personal suffering.
The groveling outrage of both poets is the result of actual or
imagined prosecution by their enemies. Hipponax pictures himself

as a victim of stoning (32 D.^{3} = 37 W.); Callimachus, as captured and bound by his own friends who have become persuaded that he is insane (203.19-21).

Both Callimachus and Hipponax then share a cluster of attitudes which are interdependent. They perceive their own virtues as unrewarded, indeed they are misunderstood and attacked. The poets take it badly; decry the injustice of it all; pity themselves and in their outrage, attack the attackers with blunt and un-compromising obscenity in the case of Hipponax, with great wit and more urbane obscenity on the part of Callimachus.

The difference in the language of their anguish and of their attack has tended to obscure the great similarity in their view of themselves at odds with their world. Callimachus, in *Iamb* 13 portrays his own contemporaries as complaining that he did not follow his Ephesian model closely enough. They say that he uses too many different dialects (203.17-18) and that he writes in the style of too many different genres (*Dieg.* IX 33-36). Although the fragments of Hipponax have metrical diversity, including pure iambic trimeters, epodes, tetrameters and even hexameters along with the choliambs, Callimachus' insistence on a metrical, dialectical and thematic mix within a collection of iambic poems has a better-known ancestor in the work of Archilochus.

Archilochus

Archilochus also shares the basic constellation of attitudes described above. He too is a wasp in Callimachus' own estimation,[13] who stings his opponents such as Lykambes (88 D.^{3} = 172 W.), on account of his outrage at being wronged (66 D.^{3} = 126 W.), which also causes acute bouts of self-pity (104 D.^{3} = 193 W.). Indeed, as Archilochus predates Hipponax by a century or so, and was credited in antiquity with the invention of the iamb,[14] we may say that it was he, as far as we know, who pioneered the use of the iambic genre as an expression of just these attitudes.

In addition to invective, the extant fragments of Archilochus also contain a great deal of other material such as animal fables, snatches of narrative, descriptions of landscape and people etc. In view of this variety it is necessary to seek a wide definition

---

[13] Fr. 380. 1-2.
[14] Clement of Alexandria *Strom.* 133.

of the term *iambos*. One particularly interesting attempt to do this has been made by K. J. Dover who suggests that Archilochus may have

> ... Used the word ἴαμβοι with reference to all the forms of poetry which he composed, their common characteristic being not their meter or language, but the type of occasion for which they were composed, their "social context" in fact.[15]

In an attempt to clarify this definition, Dover has classified Archilochus' poems not in the traditional fashion, according to their meter, but according to a typology established for pre-literate cultures. He defined seven such categories of songs which are illustrated with numerous examples from Archilochean fragments. Many of these types appear in the *Iambi* of Callimachus as well. Dover's first type of pre-literate song is the archetype for the "iambic attitude" of Archilochus, Hipponax and Callimachus. It is a song which expresses an emotional reaction of an event. The reaction may be fear, shame, rage or despair; the singer may boast, he may lament his rejection in love, or deplore his sexual inadequacy; he may also commiserate with himself, or reproach and ridicule himself, his soul, or guardian spirit or other people. Other categories include narratives about events which took place in the past, songs addressed to specific individuals, songs in which the author adopts the personality and viewpoint of another person or persons, tales wholly or partly imaginative, songs referring to sexual relationships with precise physical references made in oblique and symbolic language and finally, songs in which animals or plants are made to possess personalities of their own. Examples can be found for each of these categories in the extant fragments of both Archilochus and Callimachus.

If the term *iambos* originally covered all of these various kinds of songs, it became identified with specifically invective poetry only gradually. This narrowing of application may have been given considerable impetus by Archilochus' personal reputation for effective invective, and by the time of Hipponax the process would have been complete. While Callimachus makes use of invective and the concomitant expressions of self-justification and self-pity, his Hellenistic penchant for *poikilia* prompted him

---

[15] K. J. Dover, "The Poetry of Archilochus," *Archiloque*, Fondation Hardt Entretiens 10 (Genève 1963) 189.

to imitate the archaic variety of Archilochus. Some of the forms Callimachus uses, such as the animal fable of *Iamb* 2, have their analogue in Archilochus, while others, such as the birthday song of *Iamb* 12 are relative newcomers on the literary scene.

Aristophanes

The iambic personality which Callimachus has borrowed from Hipponax and Archilochus expresses itself in the first person singular. That first person in Archilochus and Callimachus is identified as a poet on several occasions. Archilochus says,

εἰμὶ δ᾽ ἐγὼ θεράπων μὲν Ἐνυαλίοιο ἄνακτος
καὶ Μουσέων ἐρατὸν δῶρον ἐπιστάμενος,

I am a servant of Lord Enualios
and I understand the lovely gift of the Muses.

$$(\text{I D.}^3 = \text{I W.})$$

Callimachus says that he lost Euthydemos because he "nodded" to the Muses (193.38-39), i.e. because he was a poet. It would be logical then that the critical iambicist would abuse poetry and other poets along with everything else that passed before his eye. In the extent fragments of Archilochus and Hipponax there are no examples of this. For a predecessor for Callimachus' criticism of poetic style in the *Iambi*, we must look to Aristophanes.

Comparisons between the *Aitia* prologue and the *Frogs* indicate that both Aristophanes and Callimachus used a common language of literary criticism which closely resembles what is found in later rhetorical handbooks.[16] Only three of these terms turn up in the *Iambi*. For Aristophanes as for Callimachus literary art is a τέχνη (*Ra* 785-786; 202.56) and the poet is a craftsman (*Ra.* 799-802; 814-829; 881; 902; *Dieg.* IX 36-38). Bad poets chatter (λαλέω) like Euripides in *Frogs* (*Ra.* 91; 839; 954) and Euhemerus in the *Iambi* (191.11; 192.14).

Aristophanes' most effective method of literary criticism is not the use of technical terms, but the ancient art of parody. Parody in Greek literature has a long tradition, beginning, as

---

[16] D. L. Clayman, "The Origins of Greek Literary Criticism and the *Aitia* Prologue," *Weiner Studien* 90 (1977) 27-34. J. D. Denniston, "Technical Terms in Aristophanes," *CQ* 21 (1927) 113-121. Whether the technical terms of literary criticism originated with the poets or the handbooks is a debatable point.

far as we know, with the lost *Margites* which was generally attributed to Homer and was known to Archilochus.[17] Athenaeus
(698B) claims that Hipponax was the inventor of parody and
quotes four hexameter lines which curse a lady glutton in Homeric
diction (77 D.[3] = 128 W.).[18] While the origin of the genre is clearly
older than Hipponax, Athenaeus' mistake indicates that Hipponax
had quite a reputation in this area.

The pre-eminent literary parodists in the fifth century were
the tragic poets whose satyr plays spoofed their own tragedies
and the comic poets, especially Aristophanes whose judicious
use of tragic diction in very untragic situations creates many of
the best moments in his comedies. Extended parodies of tragedy
and tragedians can be found in the *Thesmophoriazusae* (846-928;
1017-1135) where he reproduces sections of Euripides' *Helen* and
Andromeda, which had only lately been presented in the Theater
of Dionysus, and in the *Frogs* (830-1533) where Aeschylus and
Euripides contest with one another in the presence of Dionysus.

Aristophanes also parodies other literary forms, most notably,
the formal rhetorical style which was dazzling Athens at the time.[19]
The most elaborate examples of parodied rhetoric are the debates
between Just and Unjust Reasoning and between Pheidippides
and his father Strepsiades in the *Clouds* (961-1104; 1353-1451).
Unjust Reasoning, which represents Sophistic thought and supports
rhetorical education, might be expected to speak like a professional
orator, as would Pheidippides, who has undergone formal rhetorical
training in the school of Socrates. Aristophanes' comic genius
prompted him to make the speeches of Just Reasoning, which
defends the old school of education, and Strepsiades, who dropped
out of Socrates' school for lack of brain power, to speak in the
same formal fashion, adding an extra dimension to the parody.
Each of their speeches is divided into the customary parts: προοίμιον,
πίστεις, and ἐπίλογος,[20] with phrases such as the orators use to
mark the divisions or to make emphasis.[21] They use proper παρα-

---

[17] L. Radermacher, *RE* 14 (1930) 1705.

[18] Fragments in P. Brandt, *Corpusculum Poesis Epicae Graecae Ludibundae*
1 (Leipzig 1888).

[19] C. T. Murphey, "Aristophanes and the Art of Rhetoric," *HSPC* 49
(1938) 69-113.

[20] Murphey, above n. 19, 104 ff., The speech of Strepsiades also has a
diegesis (*Nub.* 1354-1376).

[21] Murphey, above n. 19, 84 lists the following words: ἐγὼ φράσω (*Nub.*
1354); πρῶτον (*Nub.* 963); εἶεν (*Nub.*1075); σκέψαι (*Nub.* 1043, 1071);
φέρε (*Nub.* 1088).

δείγματα: Just Reasoning points to the example of Heracles (1047-52) and Unjust Reasoning to Nestor and Peleus (1055-57; 1063-1066); Sophistic commonplaces, such as the praise of the powers of speech (1399-1405; 1036-42); and typical Sophistic arguments such as the argument of expediency, τὸ συμφέρον (1060-1082).

These parodies of rhetorical style can be compared with Callimachus' parody of rhetoric in the fourth *Iamb*. Both poets recreate the form and simultaneously devalue it by giving it inappropriate contents. By making his speakers talking trees, Callimachus returns in spirit to the earliest animal parodies. The Hipponactean Cynic of *Iamb* 1 and the erotic choliambographer of *Iamb* 3, are more Aristophanic in conception. Other parodies in the *Iambi* are more difficult to categorize because there are fewer fragments. *Iamb* 5 seems to be, on one level at least, a take-off on Hipponax, while *Iamb* 6 is a perverted *propemptikon* and bizarre *ekphrasis*, if not an elaborate spoof on technical didactic poetry. The extended epigrams certainly imply a jaundiced view of the literary form on which they are based, and one can imagine what Callimachus might have done with an *epinicion*.

Callimachus, then, takes the moralistic iambic persona of Archilochus and Hipponax and makes him literate. He takes aim at specific individuals such as Philton and Eudemos of *Iamb* 2, and also at generic styles, which are dissected through parody in the manner of Aristophanes. This combination of social, moral and literary criticism will later prove to be one of the most important contributions the *Iambi* make to Roman literature.

CHAPTER THREE

CALLIMACHUS AND OTHER HELLENISTIC IAMBI

With the general revival of poetry in the third century, we find that Callimachus is not the only poet who rediscovered Hipponax's choliambs. Several papyri dating from this period contain what appear to be anthologies of choliambic verse dealing with popular moral themes. An interesting example is P. Heid. 310 which contains sections of three poems: the first, attacking avarice, the second on the misuse of wealth, and the third against pederasty.[1]

The first poem shows some want of skill in metrical composition, but represents well enough the typical contents of a moralizing choliamb. As the papyrus fragment begins, the poet is railing against greedy people who have no fear of the goddess Dike (34-38). The subject of faithlessness, ἀπιστίη, appears at line 41. In line 45-46 the poet congratulates himself on his own abstemious eating habits and in lines 47-48 tells the reader in graphic terms why they should not be gluttonous. Towards the end the poet professes faith in a god who gives each man his due and concludes with a proverb (67-73).

The remains of the third poem on P. Heid. 310 are very few, but it is clear from line 120, καλὸς κίναι[δος, that the topic is paederasty.[2] πλου[on line 117 indicates that wealth was a related issue. προγάστωρ "pot-bellied" (126), ἀκρα[τὴς "intemperate" (127); σιμὸς φαλ[α]κρός "a bald-headed monkey" (131) and γλ[α]υκὸς μελαγ[χ]ρή[ς "dark-gray skinned" (132) suggest the treatment given the topic here.

There are some general similarities between the first anonymous choliamb and Callimachus' third *Iamb* on Euthydemos. Faithfulness, especially Euthydemos' lack of it is Callimachus' main subject. The gods in whom the anonymous choliambographer put his faith are in Callimachus' poem also, but there they have failed to take action (193.32). Both poems end with proverbs. On one level, then, Callimachus' third *Iamb* resembles a typical

---

[1] Text and commentary G. Gerhard, *Phoenix von Kolophon* (Leipzig 1909) 4-7 and 11-155, = fr. 1 D.³.

[2] Gerhard, above n. 1, 140 ff.

choliambic poem like the first anonymous fragment, but it soon becomes clear that the situation which motivated Callimachus' poem is a homosexual relationship—a feature of the corrupt present which is castigated in the third fragment of *P. Heid.* 310 and no doubt elsewhere in moralizing choliambic poetry which was strongly influenced by Cynic thought. Appreciation of this irony depends on a knowledge of typical choliambic *topoi* and it illustrates the literate quality of Callimachus' humor.

Elsewhere Callimachus uses the *topos* and language of the third fragment in a more straightforward manner. The *Dieg.* to *Iamb* 4 tells us that the poet was contending with one of his rivals when a third party broke in on them and put himself forward as the equal of both (VII 2-5). Callimachus calls him a Thracian and a boy-snatcher (VII 5-6). The Thracian poets Orpheus and Thamyris are both reputed to have invented paederasty.[3] In keeping with the language of the third choliambic fragment, the *Dieg.* gives the interloper's name as Simos. *Iamb* 5 is also an attack on a paederast, the school-teacher, and *Iamb* 9, the ithyphallic Hermes, ends with one.

The second of the three poems on *P. Heid.* is identified as the work of Phoenix of Colophon, a contemporary of Callimachus whose choliambs are quoted several times by Athenaeus.[4] The poem is addressed to one Poseidippos, who might be the well-known epigrammatist who is identified by the scholiast as one of the Telchines addressed by Callimachus in the *Aitia* prologue.[5] The poet complains that the rich lavish all their wealth on elegant houses but ignore their souls. Their houses are costly but they themselves are not worth three coppers.

The fragments of Phoenix preserved by Athenaeus are more interesting to us. Fragment 2 D.[3] e.g., the Epitaph of Ninus, begins with the introduction of the subject, a wealthy Assyrian (1-3). He failed to follow religious custom, we are told, and did no service to his community (4-8), but gave himself over to food, drink, and sex (9-10). The poem concludes with an epitaph in which he declares that his enemies made off with his riches (20-21) and in death his former wealth avails him nothing (13-24).

The Epitaph of Ninus is an example, on a modest scale, of

---

[3] See above p. 23, n. 33.
[4] Gerhard, 177-202 = frr. 2-6 D.[3].
[5] Gerhard, 103-104.

the extended epigram motif which Callimachus adapts in his own *Iambi*. Here the monument makes only a short address with a serious moral point. The closest parallel in Callimachus' *Iambi* is *Iamb* 11, the epitaph of Connarus. Connarus' epitaph must have been much longer, and far from having a serious moral purpose, if we can judge from the *Dieg.*, the story it told was bawdy and entertaining.

While *Iamb* 11 is closest in form to the Ninus poem, Pfeiffer points out two verbal reminiscences of it in Callimachus' first *Iamb*. The first line of *Iamb* 1,

> Ἀκούσαθ' Ἱππώνακτος· οὐ γὰρ ἀλλ' ἥκω
>
> (191.1)

seems to condense the opening lines of the epitaph itself,

> Ἄκουσον, εἴτ' Ἀσσύριος εἴτε καὶ Μῆδος
> εἶς ἢ Κοραξὸς ἢ ἀπὸ τῶν ἄνω λιμνῶν
> <Σ>ινδὸς κομήτης· οὐ γὰρ ἀλλὰ κηρύσσω.
>
> (3.13-15 D.³)

In bringing back the ghost of the dead man himself to speak these words, Callimachus is carrying the motif of the grave inscription one absurd step further.

Similarly, Ninus is introduced,

> Ἀνὴρ Νίνος τις ἐγένετ', ὡς ἐγὼ 'κούω,
> Ἀσσύριος, ὅστις εἶχε χρυσίου πόντον
>
> (3.1-2 D.³)

and Bathycles,

> ἀνὴρ Βαθυκλῆς Ἀρκάς — οὐ μακρὴν ἄξω,
> ὦ λῶστε μὴ σίμαινε, καὶ γὰρ οὐδ' αὐτός
> μέγα σχολάζ[ω]· δ[ε]ῖ με γὰρ μέσον δινεῖν
> φεῦ φ]εῦ Ἀχέρο[ντ]ος — τῶν πάλαι τις εὐδαίμων
> ἐγένετο, πά[ν]τα δ' εἶχεν ...
>
> (191.32-36)

In another fragment (5 D.³) Phoenix tells a version of the story of the Seven Wise Men as Callimachus does in *Iamb* 1.

Phoenix's life is usually dated by his reference to the destruction of Colophon by Lysimachus (Paus. 1.9.7) which occurred in 302 or 294 B.C. If these dates correspond roughly with his floruit,

Phoenix lived about one generation before Callimachus. He must have had a considerable reputation in Alexandria to merit Callimachus' attention, yet he is not the poet Callimachus is. As far as we can tell from the fragments Phoenix wrote in only one dialect, a literary Ionic. His vocabulary is comparatively unimaginative. Although he uses expressions here and there that suggest the influence of Hipponax,[6] his metrical practice is based on the precedents of Attic old comedy,[7] and in no way influenced Callimachus.

Another contemporary composer of iambi and meliambi is Cercidas of Megalopolis whom we know from *P. Oxy.* 1082 and nine miscellaneous fragments.[8] His poems are also filled with moralistic themes such as the uneven distribution of wealth and the unfortunate results of luxurious living. Cercidas' diction contrasts sharply with Phoenix's, suggesting comedy in its exuberant inventiveness. He is particularly fond of new words and new compounds, which is a trait exhibited by the laurel in Callimachus' fourth *Iamb.*[9] Cercidas' dialect is literary Doric; his principle meter, the meliamb.[10]

There is good evidence that Cercidas was a follower of the Cynic school,[11] and this fact in turn reinforces the idea that the moralizing choliambs of this period are related to a prose form known as the Cynic diatribe. The diatribe was a kind of popular moral literature the origins of which are frequently sought in

[6] J. U. Powell and E. A. Barber, *New Chapters in the History of Greek Literature,* 1st series (Oxford 1921) 16 n. 1 for a list of expressions borrowed from Hipponax.

[7] A. D. Knox, *Herodes, Cercidas and the Greek Choliambic Poets* (Cambridge, Mass. 1961) xvi.

[8] T. Bergk, *Poetae Lyrici Graeci*[4] (Leipzig 1882) 513-515, reprinted by A. S. Hunt, *The Oxyrhynchus Papyri* 8 (London 1911) 50-51, = frr. 6-8, 10-11b D.[3]. Cercidas can be given a date by a reference in fr. 2 to the death of Diogenes (323 B.C.) as a not very recent event and by allusions to Zeno (335-263 B.C.) in fr. 4 and to his pupil Sphaerus, who lived at least until 221 B.C., in fr. 5. Hunt, 26.

[9] There is a list of choice Cercidean compounds in Hunt, above n. 3, 27.

[10] The meliamb has been analyzed in a variety of ways. Hunt, above n. 3, 23 describes it as dactylo-epitritic and this view is now generally accepted. Earlier, P. Maas, "Cercidae Cynici Meliambi Nuper Inventi κωλομετρίᾳ Instructi," *Berliner philologische Wochenschrift* 31 (1911) 1011-1016, described the verse as a strophic system.

[11] Especially the subscription at the end of fr. 4, *P. Oxy.* 1082.

Platonic philosophical dialogue, but which probably depends more directly on the harangues of street philosophers.[12]

The best known diatribist is Bion the Borysthenite whose work is scantily preserved for us by his follower Teles.[13] The fragments of Teles indicate that the themes which interested him are similar to those of the choliambic poets: the evils of wealth and the exaltation of poverty. They also show that the Cynics attempted to give their messages popular appeal by salting their sermons with colloquial expressions, proverbs, fables, and even mock dialogues between personifications of moral abstractions. This effective combination of seriousness and jest has become known as *spoudaiogeloion*.

Callimachus' *Iambi* seem at home in the general context of Hellenistic moralizing literature. His decrying of wealth in *Iambi* 3 and 12, his attack on a corrupt schoolmaster in *Iamb* 5 and a pimp in *Iamb* 11 fit, formally at least, into this modern moralizing trend in literature. Like the Cynics, Callimachus woos his audience with puns, parody, mock debates, ghosts rising from the dead, trees that talk, obscenity, anything, in short, that his considerable imagination could conceive. Callimachus' intent, however, is not to create legitimate diatribes and moralizing choliambs, but to parody them. Hipponax in *Iamb* 1 is an ersatz diatribist who makes fun of a poor old Cynic (191.29-30); the fables of *Iambs* 2 and 4 expose literary not moral corruption; Callimachus attacks wealth in *Iamb* 3 because his lack of it has cost him a lover. The epitaph in *Iamb* 11 tells how the pimp left his property to the populace of Selinus. Callimachus' *Iambi* would not have met with the approval of Bion or Phoenix.

Other unmoralistic iambi were written at the time by Herodas.[14] The *Mimiambi* are a different species altogether, in essence, slices of life, small-scale dramatic presentations of the activities of common types, based ultimately perhaps on the prose mimes of Sophron. Of these, the most interesting to us is the eighth. In spite of the lacunose text, it is possible to recognize in it a kind

---

[12] Complete discussion in A. Oltramare, *Les Origines de la Diatribe romaine* (Genève 1926).

[13] The fragments of Teles have been preserved by Strobaeus and edited by O. Hense, *Teletis Reliquiae* [2] (Tüb. 1909).

[14] Texts: W. Headlam and A. D. Knox, *Herodas* (Cambridge 1922) reprinted 1966; I. C. Cunningham, *Herodas Mimiambi* (Oxford 1971). The dramatic dates of the first, second and fourth *Mimes* all fall between 280 and 265 B.C. suggesting that Herodas was a contemporary of Callimachus. Cunningham, 2.

of literary polemic presented as an elaborate allegory. Here Herodas describes a dream in which he pits himself in a leaping contest against a group of herdsmen who are decidedly unfriendly. In the course of the proceedings the narrator allies himself with Dionysus and an irascible old man who initially attacks him. At the conclusion, the narrator interprets the dream himself; although the critics will tear his poems apart, ultimately he will have great glory from them.

In order to understand Herodas' point one would like to know the identity of the old man and of the poet's critics. They are not named in our present text and in the absence of scholia one can only guess at the truth. The most popular choice for the old man is Hipponax. Other suggestions include Philitas, and Callimachus himself.[15] This last choice, that of A. D. Knox, is part of a wider interpretation of the poem as a counterblast to Callimachus' *Iambi*. This argument depends on two alleged parallels between the *Iambi* and *Mime* 8 which are supposed to prove that Herodas wrote 8 after seeing the *Iambi*.[16] The parallels are frankly unconvincing. What is clear is that Herodas took Hipponax as a model for the metrics and dialect of his *Mimiambi*, and felt himself, like Hipponax, beset by his critics. It is not possible to prove that Callimachus was among Herodas' opponents in *Mime* 8 nor that Callimachus' implied criticism of others who write choliambs in *Iamb* 13 refers to Herodas.

All we can say with certainty is that Herodas, like Callimachus, seems to be anticipating criticism which will be directed at his work and defends his literary innovations in the very act of making them.

It is clear from this brief survey that Hipponax had something of a vogue in third century Alexandria. Phoenix was already using Hipponactean diction and subject matter a generation or so before Callimachus and Herodas. The precedence which Callimachus gives to Hipponax as a literary predecessor in the iambic genre depends, perhaps, less on Callimachean literary theory than on the fashion of the times.

---

[15] Hipponax has been defended most recently and convincingly by B. Veneroni, "Ricerche su due *Mimiambi* di Eroda," *Rendiconti dell' Istituto lombardo* 105 (1971) 223-242 especially 228-229. R. Herzog, "Herondea," *Philol.* 82 (1926-1927) 27-66, supports Philitas and A. D. Knox, "Herodes and Callimachus," *Philol.* 81 (1925-1926) 241-255 and "The Dream of Herodes," *CR* 39 (1925) 13-15, prefers to see Callimachus as Herodas' rival.

[16] Herodas, *Mim.* 8.4-5 and *Iamb* 194.81-82; *Mim.* 8.78-79 and *Iamb* 203.13-14.

CHAPTER FOUR

THE INFLUENCE OF THE *IAMBI* AT ROME

The true potential of the Alexandrian approach to literature was not realized in Egypt in the lifetime of Callimachus but several centuries later at Rome. Many studies have been undertaken in an effort to evaluate the ways in which the Roman poets responded to Alexandrian literature and transformed it into a new literary idiom, much as the Alexandrians themselves had transformed their own classical heritage. Since the *Iambi* have seldom been the focus of such scholarship it will be the purpose of this chapter to inquire about their fate in the Roman literary experience.

If the hallmark of Greek iambic poetry is its variety of meter and theme, the Latin iambic poets have imitated it admirably. The *Saturae* [1] of Ennius include iambic senarii, trochaic septenarii, dactylic hexameter and sotadeans. Lucilius uses the same array at first, but later restricts himself entirely to hexameters, fixing this meter as the standard for future Latin satire.[2]

Outside of satire, a good example of iambic variety can be found in the poems of Catullus which include iambic trimeters (*C*. 4; 29), catalectic iambic tetrameters (*C*. 25), and choliambs (*C*. 8; 22; 31; 37; 39; 44; 59; 60). Catullus does not reserve the term *iambi* for these particular poems, however, but seems to use it in a generic sense to indicate invective in any meter (*C*. 36.5; 40.2; 54.6).[3] The broad meaning which Catullus gives the term *iambi* agrees well with his own poetic practice. The foulest of his attacks appear in hendecasyllables (*C*. 16; 23) and elegiacs (*C*. 69; 80; 87-91) as well as choliambs (*C*. 37; 39), while abuse of a lighter sort is found in choliambs (*C*. 22; 44) as well as catalectic iambic tetrameters (*C*. 25) and elegiacs (*C*. 84).[4] To a thoroughgoing Callimachean like Catullus, then, iambic means the iambic spirit or attitude with or without the iambic meter.

---

[1] Or *Satura*, see J. H. Waszink, "Problems Concerning the *Satura* of Ennius." in *Ennius* Fond. Hardt. Entretiens 17 (Genève 1971) 102-105.

[2] C. A. Van Rooy, *Studies in Classical Satire and Related Literary Theory* (Leiden 1965) 51.

[3] All of these poems are themselves invectives written in hendecasyllables.

[4] A fuller survey of themes and meter appears in A. L. Wheeler, *Catullus and the Traditions of Ancient Poetry* (Berkeley 1934) 44-46.

While Horace's *Satires* are uniformly dactylic, his *Epodes* have proper iambic diversity. 1-10 are couplets of iambic trimeter followed by iambic dimeter; 11 combines iambic trimeter and elegiambus; 12, dactylic hexameter and dactylic tetrameter; 13, dactylic hexameter and elegiambus; 14 and 15, dactylic hexameter and iambic dimeter; 16, dactylic hexameter and iambic trimeter; and 17, stichic iambic trimeter. Like Callimachus, Horace begins his iambi with a nucleus of poems in a signature meter (*Ep.* 1-10). These are followed by a transitional poem (*Ep.* 11), like *Iamb* 5 (see pp. 29-30 above), which looks forward to the dactylic poems and back to the iambic *Epodes*. Following the transition, metrical schemes become increasingly diverse and ingenious.

In the first century A.D., iambic diversity can be found in the *Epigrams* of Martial, which include poems in dactylic hexameter, sotadean, phalaecean hendecasyllable, iambic trimeter, iambic dimeter, choliambic trimeter and, of course, elegiac distichs. *Epigram* 1.61 is an epode consisting of choliambic trimeter alternating with iambic dimeter as in Callimachus' fifth *Iamb*.

Metrical diversity goes hand in hand with variety of contents. The heterogeneity of subject matter is so pervasive that it can be glimpsed even in the few but tantalizing scraps of Ennius. These include satirical pieces making fun of such types as the glutton (fr. 1), the loiterer (fr. 5), the slanderer (fr. 8-9) and the parasite (fr. 14-19), as well as fables (Gellius 2.29.1-20), proverbs (fr. 70), and puns (fr. 59-62). In addition to these features, the fully extant poets offer us insights into their personal lives, bits of dialogue, moralizing lectures, descriptions of places, people, things and opinions on just about everything.

In this thematic mix three types that were combined to great effect in Callimachus' *Iambi* are especially prominent: moral, social, and literary criticism. Roman satire, on the whole, concentrates heavily on the moral and social issues yet Lucilius criticizes Homer (338-347 M.), mocks Ennius' tragic diction (872-873 M.) calling him an "Homerus alter" (1189 M.), and parodies Pacuvius' Aeschylean compounds (597-600, 653-657, 867, 601, 605-607 M.) while complaining of his gloomy air and tangled prologues (875 M.). Horace tells us that Lucilius attacked Accius as well (Hor. *Sat.* 1.10.53), and uses the example of Lucilius' criticism to justify his own attacks on Lucilius himself (Hor. *Sat.* 1.10.64-71). Horace makes literature and literary criticism the central theme of three of his most successful *Satires*, 1.4, 1.10, and 2.1.

Although the satires combine moral, social and literary themes, the iambic poems of Catullus, Horace and Martial present them in a fashion which is more Callimachean. Like Callimachus' *Iambi*, the Roman iambi are located by and large in the personal world of the poet who reacts to the moral, social and literary reality around him. Like Callimachus, the Roman iambographers have erotic interests and juxtapose their interpersonal relations with larger social and literary issues.

Eros in iambi, of course, goes back to Archilochus and Lykambes' daughter (Pap. Colon. 7511.1-35) and Hipponax and Arete (19, 20-21, 92, 13 D.^{3} = 12, 14, 16 W.). Callimachus' contribution is to present his erotica in elaborate literary settings. The story of Euthydemos' defection in *Iamb* 3 is prefaced with a full-blown attack on the morals of the present age and the corrupting power of money in imitation of contemporary poetry against *aischrokerdeia*, while the cast of characters apparently included a new comic *lena* in the person of Euthydemos' mother. In *Iamb* 9 the lover of handsome Philetadas is assailed by an ithyphallic Hermes who addresses a passerby in the manner of an extended epigram. The erotic schoolteacher of *Iamb* 5 is abused with oracular riddles.

These literary settings were not imitated by Catullus and Martial whose poems, with some exceptions, are much shorter, but had considerable influence among the Roman elegiac poets. Dawson [5] has pointed out the similarities between *Iamb* 3 on Euthydemos, and Tibullus 1.9, one of the Marathus poems in which the poet has been deserted by a young man for a wealthy seducer and curses the venality of his age. In another Marathus poem 1.4, Tibullus asserts the superiority of poetry and criticizes those who reject it for wealth. Dawson also notes the similarities between this poem, in which a statue of Priapus gives amatory advice, and *Iamb* 9 on the ithyphallic Herm. Finally, in 1.5.47-48 a lena is said to have introduced Delia to a rich lover as Euthydemos' mother is charged in *Iamb* 3.

The influence of Callimachus' *Iambi* can also be detected in Propertius, Book 4. H. E. Pillinger [6] has discussed similarities

---

[5] C. Dawson, "An Alexandrian Prototype of Marathus," *AJP* 67 (1946) 1-15

[6] H. E. Pillinger, "Some Callimachean Influences on Propertius, Book 4," *HSCP* 73 (1969) 171-199.

between Propertius 4.2, the Vertumnus poem, and *Iamb* 7, the aition of Hermes Perpheraios. In both poems statues describe themselves physically, mention the artist who made them and comment at length on the etymology of their names. The aitiological poems in Propertius 4 no doubt owe something to Callimachus' *Aitia*, but their juxtaposition with amatory poems, a feature which has so baffled the critics,[7] becomes more understandable in the light of the thematic mix of Callimachus' *Iambi*. Cynthia's ghost in 4.7 may owe something to Hipponax's ghost in *Iamb* 1. Finally, Propertius' penchant for introducing new literary forms into the elegies of Book 4: the epistle in 4.3, the hymn in 4.6 and 4.9, the satire in 4.8, the *paraclausithyron* in 4.9 to mention just a few,[8] may be inspired by Callimachus' expansions of the iambic genre.

The only Roman iambi long enough to attempt literary development on a par with the elegies and Callimachus' *Iambi* are the *Epodes* of Horace. Horace's avowed mentors in this genre are Archilochus and Hipponax (*Epod.* 6.11-14), yet Callimachus' influence can be found even where Horace imitates the Ionic poets most closely. In *Epode* 2 the reader is treated to an enraptured account of the joys and virtues of country living only to discover at the end (2.67) that the speaker is the usurer Alfius. K. Lachmann [9] first pointed out the relationship between this poem and Archilochus fr. 22 D.³ = 19 W.,

"οὔ μοι τὰ Γύγεω τοῦ πολυχρύσου μέλει
οὐδ' εἷλέ πώ με ζῆλος, οὐδ' ἀγαίομαι
θεῶν ἔργα, μεγάλης δ' οὐκ ἐρέω τυραννίδος·
ἀπόπροθεν γάρ ἐστιν ὀφθαλμῶν ἐμῶν."

The possessions of wealthy Gyges are not a care to me
Nor has envy yet seized me, nor am I indignant at
the works of the gods, nor do I love great tyranny,
but these things are far from my eyes.

Aristotle (*Rhet.* 3.17, 1418ᵇ30) says that these lines were spoken by the carpenter Charon. The structure of Archilochus' poem is unknown, but it seems likely that the identity of the speaker was not immediately disclosed, creating an element of surprise as in

---

[7] Pillinger, 172.
[8] Pillinger, 175.
[9] *Kleinere Schriften* ii 78.

Epode 2.[10] Thus Horace, like Archilochus, devalues the sentiments expressed in the first part of the poem by putting them in the mouth of an unworthy speaker.

E. Fraenkel's interpretation of the poem typifies the way it is usually understood,

> The spirit of *Epode* II is very different from anything likely to be found in a work of an early iambist. If we leave for a moment the mocking conclusion, we may see in this poem a fundamentally true, if slightly idealized, expression of Horace's own nostalgic longing for the life of the country-side, a longing which he shared with many of his contemporaries. ... It is right to judge the epode from the impression which it makes upon us as a whole and not to allow the balance to be completely upset by what has been called 'the Heinesque surprise at the close.' [11]

Horace may well have enjoyed the country life, but the words with which he describes it have a history of their own which must not be ignored. Wickham, in his annotated Oxford edition of 1896,[12] notes that the poet's description of country joys contains a good deal of diction borrowed from Virgil's *Georgics*. He documents no less than nine instances of borrowing which must have had a calculated effect on Horace's well-educated readers. It is clear that Horace did not intend us to think that these were his own words or his own feelings, but in the manner of Callimachus, he created a pastiche of expressions from a fashionable literary *topos*. The effect of *Epode* 2, then, is not to make one long for the country. Horace's purpose is to expose the superficiality of the "back-to-nature" fad that had seized upon the Roman intelligentsia of his day and of the poetry which expressed these stylish sentiments. The outward form of *Epode* 2 is Archilochean but the use of literary references to comment on literary and social life is clearly Callimachean.

Epode 16 is another case in point. Here Horace appears to be addressing a Roman assembly of unspecified type in order to recommend a solution to Rome's grave political difficulties.

---

[10] E. Fraenkel, *Horace* (Oxford 1966) 59-60.
[11] Fraenkel, 60.
[12] E. C. Wickham, *The Works of Horace*, I³ (Oxford 1896) 356-357.

Fraenkel [13] describes in detail how Horace uses technical terms
and formulas borrowed from the procedures of both the senate
and assembly to introduce and set forth his proposal as if it were
a realistic measure brought before a legitimate legislative body.
The proposal which the poet makes formally in lines 35 ff. is
that the entire body of citizens migrate to the Isles of the Blest,
where the land unploughed yields grain (*Epod* 16.43), goats come
unbidden to the milk pail (*Epod.* 16.49) and the ground does
not swell with vipers (*Epod.* 16.52).

Fraenkel interprets this poem as a serious attempt to revive
the Ἀρχιλόχειος χαρακτήρ, "He pretended to speak from a public
platform to his fellow citizens as if he held a place in the body
politic comparable to the place held by the Ionian poet 600 years
before." [14] In spite of the imaginary setting and the equally imaginary solution Horace offers to the state's ills, Fraenkel insists that
the poem expresses Horace's heartfelt indignation and sorrow
at the state of affairs in Rome. [15] Fraenkel concludes with a brief
discussion of the many similarities between the language of Virgil's
fourth *Eclogue* and Horace's description of the Isles of the Blest,
noting Snell's demonstration that the Virgilian passage must be
earlier, [16] but drawing no conclusions from these facts.

Taking a lesson from the *Iambi* of Callimachus, let us consider
briefly Virgil's fourth Eclogue. This is Virgil's famous "messianic"
Eclogue in which the poet foresees the arrival of a golden age of
peace and rural tranquility in which the earth will pour forth
fruits untilled, goats uncalled will bring home their milk, the herds
will not fear lions, serpent and poisonous plant shall perish and
Assyrian spice will grow everywhere (*Ecl.* 4.18-25). The new age
is associated with the birth of a child whom Virgil leaves unnamed.
Although Virgil's vision is prophetic (*Ecl.* 4.4), the new age is
to begin at once in the consulship of C. Asinius Pollio (*Ecl.* 4.4-14)
whom Virgil addresses at line 11. Pollio was consul in 40 B.C.
and with Maecenas negotiated the Treaty of Brundisium between
Octavian and Antony, which seemed at the time to promise an
end to the long years of civil war. This is surely the context in
which Virgil's poem must be understood. Virgil's vagueness about

---

[13] Fraenkel, 43-45.
[14] Fraenkel, 48.
[15] Fraenkel, 50.
[16] B. Snell, *Hermes* 73 (1938) 237 ff.

the identity of the principals is his drama, the child and the child's father, is in keeping with the oracular tone and with good politics. His use of traditional "golden-age" imagery to reflect on the hopes attending a specific political development is a departure from tradition and a creative act of considerable distinction.

In *Epode* 16 Horace takes Virgil's idea one step further, we might say, one step too far. The "golden-age" imagery, though replete with echoes of Virgil is not in itself a travesty, but the political context, aptly vague in the *Eclogue* is here blown up to enormous proportions. The utopian dream has become a piece of legislation in a formal Roman assembly. By altering the balance of Virgil's carefully presented themes, Horace has produced an iambic rendition of Virgil's poem. The motivation for Horace's poem might have been the disillusionment which followed the end of the Pax Brundisina in 38 B.C. The inspiration for it was, no doubt, Callimachus' *Iambi* where poets give advice to crowds in the language of inappropriate genres (*Iamb* 1) and golden age *adynata* appear in unexpected contexts (*Iambi* 3 and 12).

Epodes 8 and 12, the poems against Gratidia, are also clearly influenced by the *Iambi*. These are the most puzzling and most ignored of Horace's *Epodes*.[17] The silence of scholarship is largely due to their unpleasant subject matter which includes a graphic description of the decaying body of the aging meretrix. Fraenkel has little to say about them except that they are repulsive and that they resemble some Greek epigrams which have similar subject matter (A. P. 11.66-74).[18]

Callimachus' *Iambi* provide a key for understanding 8 and 12. Like Callimachus, Horace borrows a *topos* from epigrams and elaborates it in unexpected ways. Horace begins conventionally enough with an unpleasant picture of Gratidia's anatomy (*Ep.* 8. 3-10), a jibe at her approaching funeral (*Ep.* 8.11-12) and a complaint about her excessive jewelry (*Ep.* 8.13-14). He then asks a peculiar rhetorical question, "Why is it that little Stoic books love to lie among your silken pillows?" (*Ep.* 8.15-16). The moral contrast between Stoic ideals and life among Gratidia's silken pillows is not the whole point of these lines. The use of the word *libelli* suggests that the image has a literary dimension as well.

---

[17] The scholia indicate that the same Gratidia is the central character of both poems, Pseudo-Acron, ed. F. Hauthal (Amsterdam 1966) I, 497.
[18] Fraenkel, 58.

Other diction in the poem supports this view. Two adjectives which Horace uses to describe parts of the woman's body, *aridus* (*Ep.* 8.5) and *exilis* (*Ep.* 8.10), are used by Cicero in reference to meager and dry Stoic diction (*de Or.* 2.38.159; *de Fin.* 4.3.7). Another, *tumens* (*Ep.* 8.9), often refers to excess stylistic ornament, the opposite literary extreme (Quint. 8.3.18; Tac. *Or.* 18). Just as her skinny thigh (*femur exile*) is joined with swelling calves (*tumentibus suris*) so the bald diction of the Stoic *libelli* lie among the asiatic excesses of Gratidia's silk pillows. Horace himself warns against stylistic excesses of either sort (*A.P.* 27-28) while Gratidia combines the two.

Turpis and *crudus* (*Ep.* 8.6), other adjectives from the vocabulary of animal husbandry with which Horace describes parts of the poor woman's anatomy, are employed by Cicero and Persius to characterize archaic-style verse (Cic. *Or.* 47.158; Pers. 1.92), which often gapes with hiatus like Gratidia's *podex* (*Ep.* 8.5).[19] The archaic and pseudo-archaic style is often a target of Horace's criticism both in the *Satires* (*Sat.* 1.10.1 ff.) and *Epistles* (*Epist.* 2.1.66-68).

Gratidia, then, incorporates the stylistic extremities which Horace urges writers to avoid. She is a human metaphor for everything he believes is wrong in literary style. In creating Gratidia the poet has inverted a well-known rhetorical figure in which the simple beauty of the plain style is compared to that of a naturally beautiful woman. A good example of the usual mode this figure takes can be found in Cicero (*Or.* 23.78-79):

> Just as some women are said to have a natural beauty, who are adorned by the absence of adornment, so this plain way of speaking is pleasing, even though it is unornamented. For something happens in each case, so that it is more charming, but not in an obvious way. Then every apparent embellishment is removed, like pearls. Not even curling irons are applied; indeed, all cosmetics of counterfeit white and red are eliminated; only elegance and neatness remain. The language is pure and idiomatic; it is spoken clearly and distinctly; suitability is observed.

---

[19] V. Grassman, *Die erotischen Epoden des Horaz* (Munich 1966) presents information on the meaning and usage of Horace's obscene diction. He notes that there is no parallel for Horace's graphic use of *hiet* with *podex*.

The pearls which Cicero would like to see removed appear in
Ep. 8.13-14 where Horace ironically wishes that Gratidia may
wear pearls so large that they will weigh her down.[20] The cosmetics
which Cicero deplores appear on Gratidia in *Ep*. 12.9-11 where
their composition is described as *stercus crocodili* and her excessive
perspiration makes them run.[21]

I have shown elsewhere that virtually all of the details of *Epodes*
8 and 12 contribute to the picture of Gratidia, Daughter of the
Graces, as an anti-Grace embodying all of the worst in literary
taste, whom Horace cannot and will not love.[22] In the mingling
of sex and literature (*Iamb* 3), in the adaption of a *topos* from
epigrams (*Iambi* 7, 9, 11) and in the spoofing of a well-worn
literary device (*Iambi* 2, 3, 4 etc.) it is not difficult to see the
influence of Callimachus' *Iambi* in Epodes 8 and 12.

Another *Epode* with Callimachean echoes is 10, the negative-
propemptikon in which Horace wishes his enemy an ill journey
rather than a propitious one. This poem has been compared to a
similarly virulent negative *propemptikon* on the Strasburg Papyrus.[23]
The authorship of this papyrus has been much disputed between
partisans of Archilochus and Hipponax,[24] but happily this issue
is irrelevant here. For our purposes it is enough to notice how
Horace recreates the form of the Ionian iamb as Callimachus
does in Iamb 5. It is also important to note that Horace's intended
victim is given a name—Mevius and that Mevius has been identified
by Porphyrio as the talentless poet whom Virgil attacks in *Ec* 3.90.[25]

---

[20] In *Sat*. 1.10.9-10 Horace expresses the view that too much verbiage
weighs down tired ears.

[21] Neque illi / iam manet umida creta colorque / stercore fucatus crocodili
(*Ep*. 12.9-11). Color is a respected ingredient in any literary style (Cic.
Or. 3.25.96; 3.52.199), but Gratidia's is remarkable for its excessiveness
and its composition. Pliny explains that the intestines of the land crocodile
were used as medication for facial blemishes (*H.N*. 28.28.108). By substitut-
ing *stercus* for *intestina* and using *fucus* to stand for make-up in general,
Horace intends us to understand that Gratidia's color is *stercus crocodili*.

[22] D. L. Clayman, "Horace's *Epodes* VIII and XII: More than Clever
Obscenity?" *Classical World* 69 (1975) 55-61.

[23] The comparison was first suggested by the publisher of the Strasbourg
Papyrus, R. Reitzenstein, "Zwei neue Fragmenta der Epoden des Archilochos," *Sitzungsberichte der preussischen Akademie der Wissenschaften Berlin*
(1899) 857-864 and has been frequently repeated since.

[24] For a review of the literature and the evidence see O. Masson, "Les
'Épodes de Strasbourg': Archiloque ou Hipponax?" *REG* 59-60 (1946-47)
8-27.

[25] Hic est M(a)evius inportunissimus poeta, quem et Vergilius cum simili
contumelia nominat.

In his analysis of *Epode* 10, H. Fraenkel insists that Mevius' occupation is entirely irrelevant to the poem's meaning: "If the man's bad poetry were in the least relevant to the invectve, Horace would have said or implied that Mevius was a poet. There was nothing to prevent him from doing so. . . . As the Epode stands, the versifying activities of Mevius have no place in it, and they cannot be used to account for the hatred which seems to be the essence of the poem." [26]

Fraenkel's argument is based on the assumption that most of the readers of Horace's poem would not have the slightest idea who Mevius was. As regards Horace's twentieth century readers this is no doubt true. Horace however was not writing for a public so far removed from him in time and place, but for a relatively small group of literary-minded individuals such as those for whom Virgil intended his *Eclogues*. If Mevius' identity were irrelevant, Horace would have no motive for including his name at all. He could just as well have used any other name or left the victim altogether nameless. Horace did not have to say that Mevius was a poet because his readers would already have that information, and over-explicitness would ruin the effect. Horace's inspiration for the Epode's form and the naming of poets he dislikes is certainly Callimachus' *Iambi* (2 and 5).

There is much more of Callimachus in Horace's *Epodes* than is generally allowed. In *Epodes* 2, 8, 10, 12, and 16 we have found him playing Callimachean tricks with form and content, and mixing moral, social and literary themes in the manner of the *Iambi*. Horace's grouping of his Callimachean poems together with other more innovative *Epodes* which expand the genre in altogether new directions, and the orchestration of all of them into a unified *Gedichtbuch* with a carefully developed metrical scheme and an archetectonic arrangement of themes,[27] are the ultimate Callimachean touches.

The *Epodes* of Horace are not considered to be his best or most interesting poems. The Roman work which more exuberantly and successfully carries on the spirit of Callimachus' *Iambi* while radically altering the form is Petronius' *Satyricon*. Literature and *eros* have never been combined to better effect. The fragments

---

[26] Fraenkel, 27.

[27] R. Carrubba, *The Arrangement and Structure of Horace's Epodes* (Diss. Princeton) 1964.

contain sexual episodes of every variety, and like other portions of the text, they have recognizable literary underpinnings.[28] For example, a love quarrel between Encolpius and Ascyltus (*Sat.* 9.8) is organized into pairs of opposing statements with antithesis and isocolon in the manner of formal rhetorical debate.[29] The amatory scenes in Croton (*Sat.* 134.12) contain imitations of Ovid, underscored by verbal echoes of the *Amores*.[30] Encolpius denounces his impotent organ in nine "Virgilian" lines culminating in three verses taken straight from Virgil, with which he describes its failure to respond (*Sat.* 132.11).[31]

These are only three of the many literary allusions which form the dense verbal surface of the *Satyricon*:

> The *Satyricon*, both in style and in the themes of some episodes, is permeated with reminiscences of other genres and other styles, ranging, in effect, through the whole of the classical tradition. The enumeration of the categories of oratory, historiography, legal and diplomatic formulae, epic, epistolography, erotic elegy, philosophical essay, satire, romance, tragedy, and comedy probably does not exhaust the list.[32]

As in Callimachus' *Iambi* Petronius' preferred mode of literary allusion is parody. Content is totally divorced from form and no genre is left intact. In Callimachus' *Iambi* the chaos of genre reflects the state of literature after the end of the classical period when no progress seemed possible without dissection, analysis, and ultimately, reconstruction of the old forms. In the *Satyricon* the chaos of genre is connected with a greater chaos of plot and character which together reflect not only on the end of the Roman classical period in literature, but also on the loss of a stable social environment at Rome.[33]

This review of the influence of Callimachus' *Iambi* at Rome has been noteworthy for the absence of evidence for direct borrowings from the *Iambi* by Roman poets. This should not be surprising

---

[28] C. Gill, "The Sexual Episodes in the Satyricon," *CPh* 68 (1973) 172-185.

[29] P. G. Walsh, *The Roman Novel* (Cambridge 1970) 87.

[30] J. P. Sullivan, *The Satyricon of Petronius: A Literary Study* (Bloomington and London 1968) 189-90.

[31] Gill, 178.

[32] F. Zeitlin, "Petronius as Paradox," *TAPA* 102 (1971) 648. For a complete list see A. Collignon, Étude sur Pétrone (Paris 1892).

[33] Zeitlin, 676-681.

since the remains of the *Iambi* are so few and so fragmentary. We can surmise from Martial who places a birthday song (4.45) and a portrait of a Cynic in a threadbare cloak (4.53) shortly after an elegant compliment to Callimachus (4.23) that borrowings indeed exist. If only we had more of the *Iambi* we would be able to recognize them. Their absence, in any case, is no measure of the influence of Callimachus' *Iambi* at Rome.

BIBLIOGRAPHY

PAPYRI

PSI 1094. Ed. G. Vitelli. *Papiri della società italiana* 9 (1929) 157-164.
PSI 1216. Eds. M. Norsa and G. Vitelli. *Papiri della società italiana* 11 (1935) 123-128.
P. Med. 18. Eds. M. Norsa and G. Vitelli. Διηγήσεις *di poemi di Callimaco in un papiro di Tebtynis*. Papyri della R. Università di Milano (Firenze 1934).
P. Oxy. 661. Eds. B. P. Grenfell and A. S. Hunt. *The Oxyrhynchus Papyri* 4 (1904) 62-64.
P. Oxy. 1011. Ed. A. S. Hunt. *The Oxyrhynchus Papyri* 7 (1910) 15-82.
P. Oxy 1363. Eds. B. P. Grenfell and A. S. Hunt. *The Oxyrhynchus Papyri* 11 (1915) 90-92.
P. Oxy. 2171. Ed. E. Lobel. *The Oxyrhynchus Papyri* 18 (1941) 56-62.
P. Oxy 2215. Ed. E. Lobel. *The Oxyrhynchus Papyri* 19 (1948) 38-41.
P. Oxy 2218. Ed. E. Lobel. *The Oxyrhynchus Papyri* 19 (1948) 97-98.
P. Ryl. 485. Ed. C. H. Roberts. *Catalogue of the Greek Papyri in the John Rylands Library* 3 (1938) 97-98.
P. Mich, inv. 4947. Ed. C. Bonner. "A New Fragment of Callimachus," *Aegyptus* 31 (1951) 133-137.

TEXTS OF THE IAMBI AND DIEGESEIS

Cahen, E. *Callimaque* (Paris 1922).
Dawson, C. M. "The *Iambi* of Callimachus," *Yale Classical Studies* 11 (1950) 1-168.
Gallavotti, C. *Callimaco: Il libro dei Giambi* (Napoli 1946).
Lobel, E. "The Choliambi of Callimachus in P. Oxy. 1011," *Hermes* 69 (1934) 167-178.
Lobel, E. "Callimachea II. The Trochaic Poem in P. Oxy. 1011," *Hermes* 70 (1935) 42-45.
Pfeiffer, R. *Callimachus*. 2 vols. (Oxford 1949-1953).
Pfeiffer, R. *Callimachi Fragmenta Nuper Reperta* [2] (Bonn 1923).
Schneider, O. *Callimachea* [2] (Leipzig 1870-1873).
Trypanis, C. A. *Callimachus: Fragments*, Loeb Classical Library (Cambridge, Mass. 1958).
Vogliano, A. Ed. *Papyri della R. Università di Milano* 1 (1937) 66-173.

TEXTS OF OTHER AUTHORS

Barber, E. A. *Sextii Properti Carmina* 2nd ed. (Oxford 1960).
Bergk, T. *Poetae Lyrici Graeci* [4] (Leipzig 1882).
Cunningham, I. C. *Herodas Mimiambi* (Oxford 1971).
Diehl, E. *Anthologia Lyrica Graeca* [3] (Leipzig 1949-1952).
Fordyce, C. J. *Catullus* (Oxford 1961).
Gerhard, G. A. *Phoenix von Kolophon* (Leipzig 1909).
Headlam, W. and Knox, A. D. *Herodas* (Cambridge 1922) reprinted 1966.
Hense, O. *Teletis Reliquiae* [2] (Tüb. 1909).
Kiessling, A. - Heinze, R. *Q. Horatius Flaccus: I Oden und Epoden* [13] (Berlin 1968); II *Satiren* [7] (Berlin 1959); III *Briefe* [6] (Berlin 1959).

Kroll, W. *C. Valerius Catullus* [4] (Stuttgart 1960).
Marx, R. *C. Lucili Carminum Reliquiae* (Leipzig 1904-1905).
Masson, O. *Les Fragments du Poète Hipponax* (Paris 1962).
Müller, K. *Petronii Arbitri Satyricon* (Munich 1961).
Postgate, J. P. *Tibulli Aliorum Carminum Libri Tres* (Oxford 1915).
Radermacher, L. *Aristophanes' Frösche* (Wien 1921).
Snell, B. *Pindari Carmina cum Fragmentis. Epinicia* [4] (Leipzig 1964); *Fragmenta* [3] (Leipzig 1964).
Vahlen, G. *Ennianae Poesis Reliquiae* [3] (Leipzig 1928).
West, M. L. *Iambi et Elegi Graeci* I (Oxford 1971).
Wickham, E. C. *The Works of Horace* I[3] (Oxford 1896).
Wyss, B. *Antimachi Colophoni Reliquiae* (Berlin 1936).

GENERAL

Ardizzoni, A. "Callimaco Ipponatteo," *Annali della facoltà di lettere filosofia e magistero dell' Università di Cagliari* 28 (1960) 7-20.
Ardizzoni, A. "Considerazioni sulla struttura del libro dei *Giambi* di Callimaco," *Miscellanea di studi alessandrini* in memoria di Augusto Rostagni (Torino 1963) 257-262.
Barber, E. A. "Alexandrian Literature," *The Hellenistic Age* (New York 1968, first printed 1925) 31-78.
Barber, E. A. "New Light on Callimachus," *Classical Review* 49 (1935) 176-177.
Barber, E. A. "Notes on the *Diegeseis* of Callimachus," *Classical Quarterly* 33 (1939) 65-68.
Bartoletti, V. "L'Allegoria del fuoco nei *Giambi* di Callimaco," *Studi italiani di filologia classica* N.S. 10 (1932-33) 223-229.
Bayet, J. "Catulle, la Grèce et Rome," in *L'Influence grecque sur la Poèsie latine de Catulle à Ovide*, Fond. Hardt. Entretiens 2 (Genève 1953).
Bevan, E. "Hellenistic Popular Philosophy," *The Hellenistic Age* (New York 1968, first printed 1925) 79-107.
Blass, F. "Die neuen Fragmenta griechische Epoden," *Rheinisches Museum* 55 (1900) 341-347.
Braga, D. *Catullo e i poeti greci* (Messina 1950).
Brink, C. O. "Callimachus and Aristotle," *Classical Quarterly* 40 (1946) 11-26.
Brink, C. O. "Hellenistic Worship of Homer," *American Journal of Philology* 93 (1972) 547-567.
Buck, C. D. "The Dialect of Cyrene," *Classical Philology* 41 (1946) 129-134.
Bühler, W. "Archilochos und Kallimachos," in *Archiloque*, Fond. Hardt Entretiens 10 (Genève 1963) 225-247.
Cahen, E. *Callimaque et son Oeuvre poétique* (Paris 1929).
Cahen, E. "L'Oeuvre poétique de Callimaque: Documents nouveaux," *Revue des Études grecques* 48 (1935) 279-321.
Capovilla, G. *Callimaco*, Studia philol. 10 (Roma 1967).
Capovilla, G. "Callimaco e Cirene storica e mitica," *Aegyptus* 43 (1963) 141-191, 356-383.
Clausen, W. "Callimachus and Latin Poetry," *Greek, Roman and Byzantine Studies* 5 (1964) 181-196.
Clayman, D. "Horace's *Epodes* VIII and XII: More than Clever Obscenity?" *The Classical World* 69 (1975) 55-61.
Clayman, D. "Callimachus' thirteenth *Iamb*: The Last Word," *Hermes* 104 (1976) 29-35.

Clayman, D. "The Origins of Greek Literary Criticism and the *Aitia* Prologue," *Weiner Studien* 90 (1977) 27-34.

Coppola, G. *Cirene e il nuovo Callimaco*. R. Accademia delle scienze dell'
Istituto di Bologna. Classe di scienze morali (Bologna 1935).

Couat, A. *Alexandrian Poetry under the First Three Ptolemies*, with a supple-
mentary chapter by E. Cahen. Trans. James Loeb (New York 1931).

Daly, L. W. trans. *Aesop Without Morals* (New York 1961).

Dawson, C. M. "An Alexandrian Prototype of Marathus?" *American
Journal of Philology* 67 (1946) 1-15.

Degani, E. "Note sulla fortuna di Archiloco e di Ipponatte in epoca
ellenistica," *Quaderni Urbinati di Cultura Classica* 16 (1973) 79-104.

Denniston, J. D. "Technical Terms in Aristophanes," *Classical Quarterly*
21 (1927) 113-121.

Deubner, L. "Ein Stilprinzip hellenistischer Dichtkunst," *Neue Jahrbücher
für das klassische Altertum* 47 (1921) 371-374.

Diehl, E. "Zum Hermes Perpheraios von Ainos," *Rheinisches Museum* 92
(1943) 177-179.

Diller, H. "Zu Kallimachos," *Hermes* 90 (1962) 119-121.

Dover, K. J. "The Poetry of Archilochus," in *Archiloque* Fond. Hardt.
Entretiens 10 (Genève 1963) 181-212.

Erbse, H. "Zum Apollonhymnos des Kallimachos," *Hermes* 83 (1955)
411-428.

Fiske, G. C. *Lucilius and Horace*. University of Wisconsin Studies in Language and Literature 7 (Hildersheim 1966).

Fraenkel, E. "An Epodic Poem of Hipponax," *Classical Quarterly* 36 (1942)
54-56.

Fraenkel, E. *Horace* (Oxford 1966) first published 1957.

Fraser, P. M. *Ptolemaic Alexandria* (Oxford 1972).

Gallavotti, C. "Il libro dei *Giambi* di Callimaco," *Antiquitas* 1 (1946) 11-22.

Gallavotti, C. Rev. of R. Pfeiffer, *Callimachus* II in *La Parola del Passato*
(1953) 464-471.

Gill, C. "The Sexual Episodes in the Satyricon," *Classical Philology* 68
(1973) 172-185.

Haupt, M. *Catullus qua Arte Poetas Expressit Alexandrinos* (Berlin 1855).

Hendrickson, G. L. "Archilochus and the Victims of his Iambics," *American
Journal of Philology* 46 (1925) 101-127.

Herter, H. "Bericht über die Literatur zur hellenistischen Dichtung aus den
Jahren 1921-1935," *Jahresbericht über die Fortschritte der klassischen
Altertumswissenschaft* 255 (1937) 65-226.

Herzog, R. "Der Traum des Herodas," *Philologus* 79 (1923-1924) 386-433.

Herzog, R. "Herondea," *Philologus* 82 (1926-1927) 27-66.

Howald, E. *Der Dichter Kallimachos von Kyrene* (Zurich 1943).

Huxley, G. "Ion of Chios," *Greek, Roman and Byzantine Studies* 6 (1965)
29-46.

Jacoby, F. "Some Remarks on Ion of Chios," *Classical Quarterly* 41 (1947)
1-17.

Jung, F. *Hipponax Redivivus* (Dissert. Bonn 1929).

Kapsomenos, S. G. "Συμβουλὴ εἰς τὴν ἑρμηείαν τοῦ δευτέρου ἰάμβου τοῦ Καλλιμάχου," *Athena* 47 (1937) 28-36.

Kapsomenos, S. G. "Zum Papyrus der ΔΙΗΓΗΣΕΙΣ zu Gedichten des
Kallimachos,"*Byzantinisch-neugriechische Jahrbücher* 16 (1939-1940) 1-32.

Kapsomenes, S. G. "Zum Konnidas-Iambos des Kallimachos," *Byzantinisch-
neugriechische Jahrbücher* 16 (1939-1940) 190-191.

Kassel, R. "Kleinigkeiten zu den Kallimachos Fragmenten," *Rheinisches Museum* 101 (1958) 235-238.

Kiremidjian, G. D. "The Aesthetics of Parody," *Journal of Aesthetics and Art Criticism* 28 (1970) 231-42.

Knoche, U. *Die römische Satire* ² (Göttingen 1957).

Knox, A. D. "The Dream of Herodes," *Classical Review* 39 (1925) 13-15.

Knox, A. D. "Herodes and Callimachus," *Philologus* 81 (1925-1926) 241-255.

Knox, A. D. "The Early Iambos," *Philologus* 87 (1932) 18-39.

Knox, A. D. "On Editing Hipponax: A Palinode?" *Studi italiani di filologia classica* N.S. 15 (1938) 193-196.

Knox, A. D. *Herodes, Cercidas and the Greek Choliambic Poets*, Loeb Classical Library (Cambridge, Mass. 1961).

Körte, A. "Literarische Texte mit Ausschluss der christlichen," *Archiv für Papyrusforschung und verwandte Gebiete* 13 (1938) 78-132.

Körte, A. and Handel, P. *Die hellenistische Dichtung* (Stuttgart 1960).

Kroll, W. "Hellenistisch-römische Gedichtbüche," *Neue Jahrbücher für das Klassische Altertum* 37 (1916) 93-106.

Kuiper, K. "Le Recit de la Coupe de Bathycles dans les *Iambes* de Callimaque," *Revue des Études grecques* 29 (1916) 404-429.

Lapp, F. *De Callimachi Cyrenaei Tropis et Figuris* (Dissert. Bonn 1965).

Lavagnini, B. "Osservazioni ai *Giambi* di Callimaco," *Atti di Reale Accademia di scienze lettere e belle arti di Palermo* Ser. 3, 19 (1935) 393-402.

Legrand, Ph.-E. *La Poésie alexandrine* (Paris 1924).

Lloyd-Jones, H. "Callimachus fr. 191.62," *Classical Review* N.S. 17 (1967) 125-127.

Luck, G. "Kids and Wolves: Callimachus fr. 202.69-70," *Classical Quarterly* N.S. 9 (1959) 34-37.

Maas, P. "Cercidae Cynici Meliambi Nuper Inventi κωλομετρίᾳ Instructi," *Berliner philologische Wochenschrift* 31 (1911) 1011-1016.

Maas, P. "In Callimachi Iambos," *Studi italiani di filologia classica* 40 (1934) 97.

Maas, P. review of ΔΙΗΓΗΣΕΙΣ *di poemi di Callimaco in un papiro di Tebtynis*, M. Norsa and G. Vitelli, *Gnomon* 10 (1934) 436-439.

Maas, P. *Greek Meter*, H. Lloyd-Jones trans. (Oxford 1962).

Marconi, G. "Il proemio degli *Annales* di Ennio," *Rivista di Cultura Classica e Medioevale* 3 (1961) 244-245.

Masson, O. "Les 'Épodes de Strasbourg': Archiloque ou Hipponax?" *Revue des Études grecques* 59-60 (1946-1947) 8-27.

McKay, K. J. *The Poet at Play: Callimachos, The Bath of Pallas*. Mnemosyne Supplement 6 (Leiden 1962).

Milne, H. "A Line of the Iambi of Callimachus," *Classical Review* 46 (1932) 250.

Murphey, C. "Aristophanes and the Art of Rhetoric," *Harvard Studies in Classical Philology* 49 (1938) 69-113.

Norsa, M. and Vitelli, G. "Frammenti di Archiloco in un papiro della società italiana," *Atene e Roma* ser. 3, 1 (1933) 7-12.

Oltramare, A. *Les Origines de la Diatribe romaine* (Genève 1926).

Pasquali, G. "Sul nuovo epodo fiorentino II. Archiloco o Callimaco?" *Studi italiani di filologia classica* N.S. 3, 10 (1932-1933) 169-175.

Pelckmann, J. *Versus Choliambi apud Graecos et Romanos Historia* (Dissert. Kiel 1908).

Perry, B. E. *Studies in the Text History of the Life and Fables of Aesop*. Philological Monographs published by the American Philological Association 7 (Haverford, Pa. 1936).

Perry, B. E. "Demetrius of Phalerum and the Aesopic Fables," *Transactions and Proceedings of the American Philological Association* 93 (1962) 287-346.

Perry, B. E. *Babrius and Phaedrus*, Loeb Classical Library (Cambridge, Mass. 1965).

Pfeiffer, R. "Ein neues Altersgedicht des Kallimachos," *Hermes* 63 (1928) 302-341.

Pfeiffer, R. "Ein Epodenfragment aus den Iambenbuch des Kallimachos," *Philologus* 88 (1933) 265-271.

Pfeiffer, R. "Die neuen ΔIHΓHΣEIΣ zu Kallimachosgedichten," *Sitzungsberichte der bayerischen Akademie der Wissenschaften* (1934) 10, 1-50.

Pfeiffer, R. "Zum Papyrus mediolanensis des Kallimachos," *Philologus* 89 (1934) 384-385.

Pfeiffer, R. "Callimachus," *Proceedings of the Classical Association* 38 (1941) 7-11.

Pfeiffer, R. "The Measurements of the Zeus at Olympia," *Journal of Hellenic Studies* 61 (1941) 1-5.

Pfeiffer, R. *History of Classical Scholarship* (Oxford 1968).

Pillinger, H. E. "Some Callimachean Influences on Propertius, Book 4," *Harvard Studies in Classical Philology* 73 (1969) 171-99.

Platt, A. "Callimachus *Iambi* 162-170," *Classical Quarterly* 4 (1910) 205.

Pohlenz, M. "Der romer Gaius bei Kallimachos," *Philologus* 90 (1935) 121.

Powell, J. U. and Barber, E. A. *New Chapters in the History of Greek Literature*, first series (Oxford 1921); second series (Oxford 1929).

Puelma-Piwonka, M. *Lucilius und Kallimachos* (Dissert. Zurich 1947).

Puelma-Piwonka, M. "Kallimachos-Interpretationen," *Philologus* 101 (1957) 90-100; 247-268.

Radermacher, L. "Sardismos," *Anzeiger der K. Akademie der Wissenschaften in Wien* 59 (1922) 1-4.

Rees, B. R. "Callimachus, *Iambus* I 9-11," *Classical Review* N.S. 11 (1961) 1-3.

Reitzenstein, E. "Zur Stiltheorie des Kallimachos," *Festschrift für Richard Reitzenstein* (Leipzig-Berlin 1931) 21-69.

Reitzenstein, R. "Zwei neue Fragmenta der Epoden des Archilochos," *Sitzungsberichte der preussischen Akademie der Wissenschaften Berlin* (1899) 857-864.

Rossi, L. E. "I generi letterari e le loro leggi scritte e non scritte nelle letterature classiche," *Bulletin of the University of London Institute of Classical Studies* 18 (1971).

Rostagni, A. "Le nuovo ΔIHΓHΣEIΣ e l'ordinamento dei carmi di Callimaco," *Revista di filologia e di istruzione classica* N.S. 12 (1934) 289-312.

Serraro, G. *Problemi di poesi alessandrino: I Studi su Teocrito* (Roma 1971).

Skutch, O. *The Annales of Quintus Ennius* (London 1953).

Stroux, J. "Erzählungen aus Kallimachos," *Philologus* 89 (1934) 314-319.

Sullivan, J. P. *The Satyricon of Petronius: A Literary Study* (Bloomington and London 1968).

Susemihl, F. *Geschichte der griechischen Litteratur in der Alexandriner Zeit* (Leipzig 1891-1892).

Szabó, K. "Ein Philetas-Fragment in der Tradition des Streites mit Mimnermos," *Acta Antiqua Academiae Scientiarum Hungaricae* 16 (1968) 165-171.

Teuffel, W. S. *Geschichte der romischen Literatur*, 6th ed. by W. Kroll and F. Skutsch (Leipzig 1913-1920).

Torraca, L. *Il prologo dei Telchini e l'inizio degli Aitia di Callimaco* (Napoli 1969).

Treu, M. "Selbstzeugnisse alexandrinischer Dichter," *Miscellanea di studi alessandrini* in memoria di A. Rostagni (Torino 1963) 273-290.

Trypanis, C. A. "The Character of Alexandrian Poetry," *Greece and Rome* 16 (1947) 1-7.

Tsiribas, D. A. "Καλλιμάχου ῎Ιαμβος κατὰ Ευθυδήμου," *Athena* 59 (1955) 150-174.

Van Rooy, C. A. *Studies in Classical Satire and Related Literary Theory* (Leiden 1965).

Van Sickle, J. "Epic and Bucolic," *Quaderni Urbinati di Cultura Classica* 19 (1975) 45-72.

Veneroni, B. "Ricerche su due Mimiambi di Eroda," *Rendiconti dell' Istituto lombardo* 105 (1971) 223-242.

Waites, M. C. "Some Features of the Allegorical Debate in Greek Literature," *Harvard Studies in Classical Philology* 23 (1912) 1-46.

Walsh, P. G. *The Roman Novel* (Cambridge 1970).

Waszink, J. H. "The Poem of the *Annales* of Ennius," *Mnemosyne* series 4, 3 (1950) 215-240.

Waszink, J. H. "Problems Concerning the *Satura* of Ennius," in *Ennius* Fond. Hardt, Entretiens 17 (Genève 1971) 97-137.

Webster, T. B. L. "Sophocles and Ion of Chios," *Hermes* 71 (1936) 263-274.

Webster, T. B. L. "Chronological Problems in Early Alexandrian Poetry," *Wiener Studien* 76 (1963) 68-78.

Webster, T. B. L. *Hellenistic Poetry and Art* (London 1964).

Wehrle, F. "Apollonios von Rhodos und Kallimachos," *Hermes* 76 (1941) 14-21.

West, M. L. "Callimachus on the Pythagoreans," *Classical Review* N.S. 21 (1971) 330-331.

West, M. L. *Studies in Greek Elegy and Iambus* (Berlin 1974).

Wheeler, A. L. *Catullus and the Traditions of Ancient Poetry* (Berkeley 1934).

Wiersma, W. "The Seven Sages and the Prize of Wisdom," *Mnemosyne* series 3, 1 (1933-1934) 150-154.

Wilamowitz-Möllendorff, U. von, *Hellenistische Dichtung in der Zeit des Kallimachos* (Berlin 1924).

Wimmel, W. *Kallimachos in Rom*, Hermes Einzelschriften 16 (Leiden 1960).

Zeitlin, F. "Petronius as Paradox," *Transactions and Proceedings of the American Philological Association* 102 (1971) 631-684.

GENERAL INDEX

Accius 73
Acontius 3
Adonis 22
adynata 78
Aegina 38
Aeschylus 51, 64
Aesop 17, 20, 47
Aesopic fables 17-18, 23-24, 36, 49
αἴνιγμα 33
αἶνοι 33
Ainos 36
aischrokerdia 20, 22, 48, 66-67, 74
aitiologies 48
  aition of Hermes Perpheraios 36-38
  aition of the Hydrophoria 38-39
  aition of ithyphallic Hermes 39
  aition of swine sacrifice to Aphrodite Castnia 40
ἀκούω 46
Alcmeon 14
Alfius 75
allegory 28
Amphalces 13
Antony 77
ἀπεμπολῆ κόψας 46
Aphrodite 40, 52, 59
Aphrodite Castnia 40
Apollo 13, 24-25, 41-44, 52
Apollo Delphinius 53
Apollonius Rhodius 39
Archilochus 16, 37, 58, 61-63, 64, 65, 74, 75, 77, 80
Ardizzoni, A. 7, 53, 59
Arete 58, 74
aridus 79
Aristophanes 50, 51, 63-65
Arsinoe 52-53
Artemis 41, 44
Artemis of Eretria 40
Ascyltus 82
Aspendus 40
Athena 42
Athenaeus 64, 67

Bartoletti, V. 8
Bathycles' Cup 13-14, 17, 23, 56, 68
Bentley, R. 1, 1 n. 5, 2

Blass, F. 2
Blomfield, C. 2
Bühler, W. 31
Bion 70
birthday song 41, 48, 63, 83
bramble 23, 27-29
Branchus 6, 24, 53
Bupalus 33, 56, 58

Cahen, E. 3, 6, 8
Callimachus
  qua iambicist 58-59
  the *Iambi* (see passages cited)
    general features 48-49, 53-54
    history of text 1-10
    Iamb 1 11-16
    Iamb 2 17-20
    Iamb 3 20-22
    Iamb 4 23-29
    Iamb 5 29-33
    Iamb 6 33-35
    Iamb 7 35-38
    Iamb 8 38-39
    Iamb 9 39-40
    Iamb 10 40
    Iamb 11 40-41
    Iamb 12 41-44
    Iamb 13 44-47
    literary criticism in 65
    obscenity in 59
    relationship to the poetry of
      Archilochus 61-63
      Aristophanes 63-65
      Cercidas 69-70
      Herodas 70-71
      Hipponax 55-61
      Horace 75-81
      Martial 83
      Petronius 81-82
      Phoenix 66-69
      Propertius 74-75
      Tibullus 74
  the *Mele* 5-7, 52-54
Cassandra 33
Catullus 7, 53, 54, 74
Cercidas 69-70
Charites 35
Charitadas, son of 23, 28, 29

PASSAGES CITED

Printed in the United States
By Bookmasters